Politics, Prayer and Parliament

Tony,

With my good wish
and many thanks for 1973/74

/s in

Jah

Politics, Prayer and Parliament

DAVID ROGERS

CONTINUUM
LONDON and NEW YORK

Continuum
Wellington House, 125 Strand, London WC2R 0BB
370 Lexington Avenue, New York, NY10017 - 6550

First published 2000

British Library Cataloguing-in-Publication Data

A catalogue record for this book is available from the British Library.

Library of Congress Cataloging-in-Publication Data

Rogers, David, 1939–
    Politics, prayer and parliament / David Rogers.
      p. cm.
    Includes bibliographical references and index.
    ISBN 0-8264-5156-X (pb)
      1. Church of England. 2. Christianity and politics—Great Britain. 3. Church and
    state—Great Britain. I. Title.

BX5157.R64 2000
322′.1′0941—dc21

                                                                                  99-048976

                    ISBN 0 8264 5156 X (paperback)

Typeset by Paston PrePress Ltd, Beccles, Suffolk
Printed and bound in Great Britain by Redwood Books, Trowbridge, Wilts

Contents

Acknowledgements and Thanks

MY particular thanks to Andrew Lownie, my literary agent, and to Ruth McCurry and Diana Smallshaw at Cassell. My thanks to all those authors I have quoted and to all politicians, priests and laity I talked with concerning this book. In each case I made it clear we talked confidentially on lobby terms, but they know who they are and I am most grateful.

I am very glad to acknowledge permission to quote from George Bell's (Bishop of Chichester 1929–58) speech in the House of Lords to the Report of the House of Lords Debates (Hansard) and to the Controller of Her Majesty's Stationery Office. Also to HMSO for quotes from the House of Commons Home Affairs Select Committee; to Lord Runcie for extracts from his Falklands sermon at St Paul's; to the Writers House Literary Agency for extracts from Martin Luther King's 'I have a dream' speech; to *L'Osservatore Romano* for extracts from Pope John Paul II's speech at Czestochowa; and to Twenty-Third Publications for quoting the prayer of John D. Powers; to Charles Moore, Editor of the *Daily Telegraph*, for extensive quotes from his article, 'The Story That Will Make the Millennium' (23 April 1999).

To Erica

I

Introduction

'ANYONE who thinks that politics and religion don't mix is not reading the same Bible I am.' With those words Bishop Desmond Tutu of South Africa encapsulates the fact that throughout history the territory of politician and priest has always overlapped.

When kings in the United Kingdom were active politicians, Shakespeare, with 'Cry God for Harry, England and St George', expressed the desire of all fighting a cause to have God on their side. Over 500 years later, Margaret Thatcher was allegedly more than slightly peeved by the suggestion of the Archbishop of Canterbury that after the Falklands War the Argentine servicemen were deserving of our prayers.

The twentieth-century struggle in Northern Ireland between Protestant politicians and Roman Catholic politicians has shown both factions firmly convinced that God is on their side.

Does God take sides? If so, what criteria does he (or as some would say, she) take? If it is clear to God what is right and wrong why doesn't the power of prayer convey that message to those who invoke his name? Do those who invoke his name in favour of cancelling Third World debt, arguing for or against women priests, or in support of their particular version of saving the planet, do so because they feel this is what God is telling them to do? Or is it a more cynical exercise with people saying what they believe to be right, and then, because they have so much confidence in their own judgement, using God to add ballast to their campaign?

This is one of the main dilemmas of faith. Christians want to do God's will. As humans, by definition, are fallible creatures, how can they be sure that they are not just projecting their own desires onto God?

This is where the activity of prayer should help. There are many testaments that in private life the concentration of thought and the opening of the mind to new ideas has been a real help to those making difficult decisions: the switching off of a life-support machine, or whether or not to have an abortion. Almost every serious autobiography or biography carries examples of this magnitude.

Public prayer is of a different order. In the Church of England there is an emphasis on the common good and peace. But little about how agreement is reached on what is good – fox hunting in a rural parish? Or common – the position of women in a multiracial urban parish? And the price of peace, if not going to war means injustice, corruption or genocide, is rarely included in intercessions.

Yet public prayer is part of our life. It is the outward and visible manifestation of the nation's idea of religion. We see it in domestic and local life, at funerals and weddings, in schools, hospitals and prisons, by the work of chaplains in the armed forces. It also has a high visible profile in national life. The discussions about the role of religion in the millennium celebrations suggest that that profile may be changing, not only to the extent of the importance of the established church but also with regard to the balance between Christianity and different faiths. However, a counterpoint to this was shown at the funeral of Diana, Princess of Wales when, to the surprise of some, millions intuitively turned towards God as a cornerstone for public and private grief.

The historical accident of the establishment of the Church of England (God moving in mysterious ways!) is glossed over. The Church of England does not celebrate the fact that it came into being from a desire of a king to divorce. But the repercussions are with us still and need to be carefully explored for an understanding of the workings of public life. Most people know that the Monarch can't either be a Roman Catholic or marry one. But how many know that not only have we never had a Roman Catholic Prime Minister but also there is one Cabinet post it would be very difficult for a Roman Catholic to hold. The Lord President of the Council (Leader of either the Commons or the Lords) has to be a Church Commissioner and has a specific duty to protect the Prayer Book. ('Where were you?' someone yelled to the Lord President, Lord Whitelaw, in 1983, at a public meeting in Greenwich, when he was explaining the duties of his office. 'Why did you allow our Book of Common Prayer to be usurped by the ASB? Where was your protection?' they demanded.)

The established church and the public prayers formed by such a body are woven into our daily lives: our activities with families and friends, and the life of the nation. Those who say that the impact of the church has little to do with their lives are forgetting the Christmas rush, the wedding car, the vicar at the crematorium, the candles lit and the religious impulse which leads to flowers strewn at sites of tragedy and disaster. Those who say that God has little impact on them should pause to consider why 'Oh, my God!' is the commonest exclamation in the language. If you doubt that, just listen to the first reaction of those who have had their rooms changed by BBC Television's *Changing Rooms* or their gardens done over by *Ground Force*.

Because we have an established church, politicians and Parliament are inextricably involved in public prayer. The millennium is a natural time to take a look at this role in our growing multiracial and multicultural nation.

2

Politician and Priest

POLITICIANS and priests are like overlapping circles. At the extreme edge of the priestly perimeter men and women can live in solitude and contemplation, remote from the problems of income tax or which channel to watch on TV. In an almost mirror image some politicians will be solely concerned with the here and now. What are the votes in more taxes for health and education? Who will march to save my version of the countryside?

But move to the point where the circles overlap and there is a common ground of interest if not of agreement. Bishops become concerned not so much (it seems to some politicians) with people's spiritual well-being but with material poverty and economic opportunity. This often produces a 'get your tanks off my lawn' debate which might be great fun, but rarely does much good.

At a fringe meeting at the Conservative Party Conference at Blackpool in the 1980s Bishops Sheppard (Anglican) and Worlock (Roman Catholic) were doing their famous and well-regarded double act on the subject of world poverty. Their justification for doing so – Jesus' concern for the poor – could not be challenged. But one delegate, slightly annoyed by what she considered to be their too-confident self-belief, commented: 'Typical of church leaders. In those areas where they are meant to be expert they duck and dive and can't agree to tell us what God feels about my sex becoming priests. Yet on a subject on which they are not expert, economic affairs, they are absolutely certain they know the answer to Third World debt.'

This is not surprising. Most politicians and priests want to change the world: some in big ways, some in small. It has always been the case: extend the Holy Roman Empire; have a crusade; or an inquisition; invade Poland; stop the slave trade; open shops on Sundays; reform the law on homosexuality; save our local school.

4

Alternatively, there is just being there for people, whether elected or appointed – surgery or confessional, listening, helping. Sometimes politicians act as priests; sometimes the clergy are active in the political domain. Of course the roles overlap and some people don't welcome the confusion.

'In the beginning was the Word' (John 1:1). That is true for politician and priest. The Sermon on the Mount, the Gettysburg Address, Churchill's 'Blood, sweat and tears', Martin Luther King's 'I have a dream'. Words can mark events and present ideas which can change perceptions and result in different actions.

The importance of the 'word' is as true in our own domestic life. So many activities are marked by this: the 'words' chosen to toast the bride, to give an obituary, to salute a retirement. These are significant occasions and words are benchmarks to show that.

We know that words can move us to tears and anger even when we know that, as in plays and poems, they are fictitious. They are a powerful tool in the hands of those who wish to sway our opinions and influence our actions. This is something that priest and politician share and should be treated with great care and respect. Their words can produce joy and inspiration, but also guilt and suffering.

The pen is mightier than the sword. Possibly true. But the spoken word delivered by one who believes in what they are saying and understands how to say it is more powerful still. Hitler was more powerful than Laurence Olivier playing Henry V because he thought he knew what he was doing. Claire Bloom tells a story of going to congratulate Olivier one night after a brilliant performance which had held the theatre in the palm of his hand. She found him trashing his dressing room. 'What's the matter. You were brilliant. You had the audience just where you wanted them.' 'I know,' trembled our greatest actor in frustration, 'but I don't know how I did it.'

On the whole, the *best* performers among politicians and priests – because they believe in their words and don't need script-writers and directors – know how they achieve their effects: putting up an Aunt Sally to knock down, two negatives followed by a positive, the long pause, the change of pace.

Sermons and speeches are their main weapons. They have much in common: the opportunity in a few words to make the comfortable feel uncomfortable and the uncomfortable comfortable; a few words which can help or hinder the making of a reputation and advance or retard a career. With both professions the importance of words starts even before speeches and sermons. There is first a need to be reasonably well read before presenting oneself to a selection panel.

In the case of the church, some think there is too much emphasis on reading and that this cuts the clergy off from a large potential constituency. David Sheppard tells of the time he was priest in South London and a man wandered into his church. After what Sheppard thought was a useful chat, he expressed the hope that he might see the visitor at a service on Sunday. 'Oh no,' replied the man, 'this isn't for me.' He waved his hand around the church with the stacks of Bibles, prayer books and various hymn books – 'It's all about those who like books.' Sheppard said he then pondered about the fact that the very first thing most churches did to people when they came on Sundays was to give them at least one book, often more.

After the reading comes the words at interview: the attempt to show cleverness in manipulating a question-and-answer session. It is not just the church and politics that proceed this way. Education, industry and business all use interviewing techniques in selection. It is just that in the church and politics – unlike other jobs such as heart surgery, flying a plane or designing a building – words, expressing ideas, can become ends in themselves. Sometimes a facility with words, using wit and humour, can be a passport to progress while often covering up laziness or lack of real concern. A tutor at a theological college told me he still had doubts about being swayed by a candidate for admission, who, in the midst of a dull, boring, batch of applicants, when asked if he had read the book list replied, with just the right intonation in his voice to raise the interest of the panel, 'Oh, yes. I've read the book list.' He went on to be a glib clergyman.

Politicians are the same. It is difficult to think of one substantive measure that F. E. Smith brought forward in Parliament. But his wit is still remembered. This was the man who, after messing up his first case at the bar, was told by the judge, 'Mr Smith, I am no wiser now than when you began your summing up.' Smith immediately replied, 'Maybe not, my Lord, but much better informed.' His client's case is long forgotten; his remark is often quoted.

Some politicians, like some clergy, will say that they are not there to achieve material substance but to make people think. Enoch Powell was only a Conservative Cabinet minister for a few months, yet on the two subjects he thought vital to the future, racial harmony and the European Union, he got people assessing their opinions. Powell was controversial both as a politician and a Christian: neither glib nor shallow, considered by many to be too logical for his own good. Iain Macleod used to say, 'I travel on the same train as Enoch but I get off at a station a few stops before it hits the buffers.' Powell set Christian leaders a problem. They were quite convinced he was wrong but recognized that he was a far greater scholar than them – not many of them had learnt Hebrew so that they could deal with questions of biblical translation at first hand. He had, in common with the great preachers like Donald Soper, the ability to understand and play an audience. When heckled at Birmingham after leaving the Conservative Party and encouraging voters to support Labour, a voice yelled out, 'Judas!' With hardly a pause, Powell found the heckler in the audience, pointed at him and rejoined, 'Judas? Judas was paid. I'm making a sacrifice.'

This highlights one of the big differences between making a speech and giving a sermon: audience reaction. Apart from a very few occasions, the clergy don't get heckled. One rector said to me, in exasperation, that he sometimes wondered what on earth he would ever have to say to get a member of the congregation to get up and declare, 'Er, just a minute, I don't think I agree with that.' The clergy get little feedback. The early tradition of obedience and the still current practice of deference mean that while some people will murmur 'Very good sermon, Vicar' as they leave the church, not many will say, 'I think you got that wrong, let's have a talk about it.'

This lack of challenge can build up an arrogance so that when clergy are challenged outside of a church environment they can't cope. This is often true, according to one former producer of BBC's *Any Questions*, of those who become bishops and find themselves with a questioning audience. The compounded effect of this is that literally preaching to the converted can result in long and boring sermons. In spite of competitions to find the preacher of the year, or whatever, there are still a tremendous number of clergy who get into the pulpit, say what they are going to say, say it, then say they have said it – then repeat it. It is not surprising that games such as P. G. Wodehouse's, 'The Great Sermon Handicap', where bets are taken on the longest sermon in the district, flourish from time to time.

This is harsh. But little sensitive training is given. I once spoke to a group of students, none of whom were familiar with the maxim that if you know your subject you can speak for an hour immediately; to speak for twenty minutes will take half-an-hour's preparation; to speak for five minutes you need a whole day to get ready. At least the advent of women priests is getting rid of the dreadful clergy voice so beloved by television sitcoms.

This criticism must be tempered by the recognition of all the difficulties. To produce, in some cases, many sermons a week, with little or no feedback, can easily lull the speaker further and further into their own prejudices – or problems. David Silk, Bishop of

Ballarat, says you can always spot what is personally troubling someone if you listen carefully to the words of a sermon. It is a lonely business and loneliness can breed isolation.

Most priests, like most politicians, do not want to be cut off from the main body of opinion of their peers. 'What will the Bishop think?' is echoed exactly by 'What will the Prime Minister think?' The temptation for both is to play safe. The justification, or excuse, depending which way it is looked at, is, 'It's not my job to upset people by being a pacifist/supporting the Euro/saying I don't believe in the virgin birth/bombing Iraq/agreeing to marry divorced people in church.' Whatever. To which the response is, 'Oh, isn't it?' Politicians are often criticized for following the party line. Clergy are often seen as undisciplined individuals who will say anything.

Criticism of a different kind can be levelled at politicians' attempts at speaking in public. At least the clergy focus on a moral message; the intention is to move the hearts and minds of the audience. This is only sometimes true of the politician who needs to judge the success of a speech by the actions of the audience. Unlike the clergy, the politician gets clapped or booed; the audience, if there is one, can walk out.

This is another essential difference. The audience for the clergy is there in the pews. Unless the local church is extremely good at modern communications there won't be a report in the paper or on regional radio. The politician is speaking for a press release with at least one soundbite to be relayed to a wider audience. There may be only one person in a draughty hall to listen to an MP, but the soundbite phrase in the local paper will reach more people than an average church congregation. Not always, because competition to get soundbites reported is increasing all the time and hopefully clichés and bad puns will be those that 'fell by the wayside' (Matthew 13:3).

Now, there is a good soundbite, doing exactly what it should: staying in the minds of listeners and when remembered recalling the whole of the passage about the sower – and the point the parable was making. The Bible is full of marvellous soundbites, especially the Sermon on the Mount. We remember a few key words ('Blessed are the poor in spirit' – Matthew 5:3), and like generations before us we can re-create the sense of what Jesus was saying.

Perhaps this is a lesson for politicians and clergy alike. When you speak, even if it is not as often as your conceit would like, prepare carefully the few key words you want remembered.

It is not only public speaking that clergy and politicians have in common. They are both professionals dependent to a large extent on the effectiveness of unpaid voluntary workers. The MP may have a paid agent but it is the volunteers who provide the platform by serving on committees, delivering literature and giving donations to keep the organization in good shape. The clergy may have paid vergers, but it is the volunteers who provide the platform by serving on committees, delivering literature and giving donations to keep the organization in good shape.

In both cases, there is a structure for volunteers with ambitions to stretch their serving upwards through regional organizations (politics), diocesan structures (church), national committees (politics), General Synod (church). The professional and the volunteers are entirely co-dependent on one another. In politics, the local volunteers have an advantage over their comrades active in church affairs – though often they are the same people, even if the Church of England is very definitely no longer the Conservative Party at prayer! They have a bigger say in selecting their candidate than lay church folk have in picking their vicar. From time to time this gives rise to local tension when the MP can respond to a political attack from the pulpit by asking, 'Who elected you?' But, on the whole, relationships between professional clergy and politicians work well at local level; even if, from time to time, the Don Camillo factor can be seen.

Clergy suffer because, unlike MPs, they can't get away from their patch and empathize with their fellow practitioners for much of the week. Like MPs, all clergy have more in common with others doing the same job than with those (no matter how close and dedicated) outside. Only another MP really understands the pain of having done a marvellous constituency job for five years yet being swept away to oblivion on the tide of the national swing. Only another member of the clergy really appreciates the difficulty of being in a broken marriage, in debt, losing faith, and yet having to comfort the dying.

They also both have the problem of deciding how to treat opponents. Though clergy may not put it quite like that; and here the problem is slightly different for MPs. At Westminster they can happily mix with, pair with and be friends with members of another party. The system demands it. In the constituency they may have to face candidates from time to time, but as the sitting MP they can be graciously patronizing and not bother too much (unless they are members of the Labour and Liberal Democrat Parties whose local constituencies may well in the future become part of national horse-trading).

For the local clergy, the position is not so clear, and is changing. Only a few years ago Anglicans would feel Roman Catholics were misguided and try to win them over; and vice versa. Now most towns have a structure of churches working together, stressing the factors that are common. The church is still not sure how far this tolerance extends to other faiths, yet recognizes that at local level no good would probably be achieved by a missionary programme of conversion. Mission, where it happens at all, seems aimed at those who believe in nothing. One of the sad current truths for both church and political parties is that on the whole resources are too tightly stretched in maintaining what they have, to be able to attempt expansion. There are exceptions to this but both temporal and spiritual experience suggest that campaigns that try to recruit and fail have such a demoralizing effect on those taking part that the unspoken consensus seems to be 'Let's think very carefully about this and then not do it'.

It may well be that in both areas the way forward is not by specific projects and evangelistic campaigns but by creating situations of witness, showing warmth, life and outgoingness both from local political parties and from welcoming churches.

At local level politicians and priests are linked as professionals on their own patch in that neither has a ring-fenced job description. They both have some tasks they must do: offer the sacrament or support their party in Parliament; and things they should do, such as looking after their parishioners or constituents. And they have things they can do, which are unlimited. They can campaign for causes close to their hearts; politicians can become consultants; they can serve on advisory committees; write books or play cricket; sit in the pub. All these things they can do quite legitimately, saying they are part of their job – to be where people are, to extend their contacts and the influence of their word.

Perhaps because both jobs can be so open-ended there is more scope than in most professions for getting into trouble. Because both the politician and priest are saying 'follow me', with all the implications of knowing how to lead a good life and set an example to others, when they fall from grace they are ripe targets for media attention and especially the tabloid press. It is probably not that they sin more than the average journalist or estate agent (figures are impossible to prove anything in this case), though often the isolation of the lifestyle doesn't help. But they are vulnerable to publicity. Could the natural human desire (sometimes) to see those who tell us how to live fall off their own pedestals be part of God's gift to remind us all, collectively, that as humans we are all fallible?

One way of coping with such a disparate life is, in both cases, an element of ritual. The organization, order and familiarity of a church service is matched by the understanding and procedural formality (if not the order) of the parliamentary day. This provides a discipline – to have to say evensong, or to have to vote at ten – which is one way of keeping a physical and an emotional control.

Many people are surprised by this close link between those who practise politics and those who are priests. In his book, *Turning to Prayer*, written when Dean of King's College, London, Richard Harries, Bishop of Oxford, links politics and prayer with poetry:

> It might seem odd that in a book on prayer there is a chapter concerned with politics and poetry. Why are they included? First, because many people regard either politics or one or other of the art forms as more important than anything else in life. Politics, or music, for example, is for them a ruling passion. One of the themes of this book is that whatever matters to us, whatever we feel strongly about, needs to be integrated into our prayers. In this way our prayer will become honest and vital.

At the time of writing, at the end of the twentieth century, the formal links between religion and politics are being considered in the public domain as part of a wider constitutional debate. This includes the future of the established church and the role of the Monarchy, the Bishops and the House of Lords. But for centuries the leaders of the Church of England and our political parties have been interdependent.

At the moment it is circular and seamless: the Archbishop of Canterbury crowns the Monarch as Head of State; the Prime Minister appoints the Archbishop of Canterbury; the General Synod decides the rules of the Church of England. A Member of Parliament who is appointed a Church Commissioner answers for them in the chamber of the House of Commons. The two Archbishops, Canterbury and York, and the Bishops of London, Durham and Winchester, plus the next most senior 21 bishops, sit in the House of Lords. The two Archbishops are junior to the Peers of the Royal Blood, but senior to the Dukes, Marquises, Earls, Viscounts and Barons. In order of precedence, the Bishops – who always have to sit on the government side of the House (whatever their own political convictions) – squash in between the 104 Viscounts and the 850 or so Barons.

In the official order of precedence – i.e.

The Monarch
Prince Philip
Prince of Wales
Monarch's younger sons

Monarch's grandsons
Monarch's cousins
Archbishop of Canterbury
Lord High Chancellor
Archbishop of York
Prime Minister
Lord President of the Council
The Speaker
Lord Privy Seal

– the Archbishop of Canterbury is higher than the Prime Minister (though appointed by the PM) and the only member of the House of Lords (apart from the Royal Princes, who in practice play no part) of higher rank than the presiding Lord Chancellor. Spiritual and temporal intermingle all the way down to Members of the British Empire, with suffragan bishops – who don't sit in (and like all clergy can't stand for) Parliament – ranked higher than barons with seats in the House of Lords.

Church and state have been interwoven throughout history. The form for the opening of each day's business in the chambers of the Lords and Commons begins with prayers largely unchanged since 1660. In the Commons the Speaker's Chaplain presides; in the Lords one of the sitting Bishops. Prayers and Psalm 67 are read and no strangers are admitted to the galleries until the door-keepers shout, 'Prayers are over!'

There is a special prayer of Parliament written by an unknown author in 1661:

> Almighty God, by whom alone Kings reign, and Princes decree justice; and from whom alone cometh all counsel, wisdom and understanding; We thine unworthy servants, here gathered together in thy Name, do most humbly beseech thee to send down thy heavenly wisdom from above, to direct and guide us in our consultations: And grant that, we having thy fear always before our eyes, and laying aside all private interests, prejudices, and partial affections, the result of all our counsels may be to the glory of thy blessed Name, the maintenance of true Religion and Justice, the honour and happiness of the Queen, the publick wealth, peace and tranquillity of the Realm, and the uniting and knitting together of the hearts of all persons and estates within in the same, in true Christian Love and Charity one towards another, through Jesus Christ, our Lord and Saviour. Amen.

The only way MPs can reserve specific seats for the day's business is if they slot a prayer card into a seat before the House sits.

So inculcated are prayers as symbolic of starting the day's work in the chamber that when Cabinet ministers start their work (often at a very early hour indeed) with a staff meeting of their private office these occasions are known as 'prayers'.

Almost by definition, and certainly by observation, the thoughts of politicians on religion, and the clergy on politics, are collectively confused. Otherwise all Christians would support one political party. The fact that they don't is due to a mix of historical and environmental factors. A Roman Catholic, Humphrey Berkeley, who was a Conservative MP and later both a Labour and Liberal candidate, put it like this: 'If you live in Bournemouth, statistically you are unlikely to vote Labour. If you live in Deptford you are unlikely to be a member of the Tory Party. But the word of God reaches everywhere.' There has also been a significant class factor in the approach members of the two main political parties have had to religion. Traditionally the Conservative Parliamentary Party was drawn from the governing classes of the landed gentry, the best attracted to politics to help those not so fortunate. Viscount White-law, when asked why he entered the House of Commons, said, 'In the Second World War I saw many young boys getting themselves killed to support my way of life. I had to give something back.'

Universal franchise was started by the 1832 Act. Then MPs from the Conservative and Liberal Parties were already in situ in Parliament and needed to create local associations to support and elect them. Conditions were ripe for deference. As the Labour Party developed, their members needed to band together locally to select a candidate to become an MP. It was much more a case of being first among equals. Up until the end of the twentieth century it was this generalization – with the cross-over exceptions of working-class Tories – that, following the collapse of the Liberals over the Irish question, kept the two-party system going.

Those on the left who were Christians took the attitude of working together politically into their religious activities, most noticeably the Christian Socialists of the last century. These were a group of clergy and lay men who were inspired by a study of social conditions to put their Christianity to political effect. The novelist Charles Kingsley was a driving force in setting up a journal, *Politics for the People*. His views became more well known in his book, *Cheap Clothes and Nasty*, an attack on the sweat shops of the East end:

No man who calls himself a Christian shall ever disgrace himself by dealing at any showshop or slop shop. They are temples of Moloch.

Their thresholds are rank with human blood. God's curse is on them, and on those, who by supporting them, are partakers of their sins. Let no clergy deal at them ... It is competition that is ruining us, and competition is division, every man against his brother. The remedy must be in association, co-operation, self sacrifice for the sake of one another.

A similar strand of both thought and action was running through parts of the trades union movement, finding expression in the Methodist Church. It was no accident that the term for a companionship of workers, especially compositors in printing offices, was 'chapel'. There are good accounts of this in the recent history of Christian Socialism by Alan Wilkinson.

Later in the century, some of Kingsley's followers took up a more muscular form of Christianity and in *A History of The Church in England* J. R. H. Moorman writes: 'From 1877 onwards the Guild of St. Matthew under Stewart Headlam's leadership was in the forefront of any movement for pressing the claims of the oppressed. Riots, marches for the unemployed, even expeditions to break the windows of West-end clubs, were often led by the curate of Bethnal Green.'

The essence of this strand of Christianity was in the emphasis on the 'brotherhood of man', of human partnership, of recognizing Christ in one another. As one of their number, the lawyer J. M. Ludlow, wrote in their journal, 'Socialism is but the recoil of Individualism.'

The right of the political spectrum tended to be more concerned with a direct personal spiritual relationship with God. Many commentators have argued that was only to be expected. Paul Filmer says, 'in the same way that they had the time and money to be patrons of the arts, so they had the leisure to indulge in prayer and worry about their spiritual well being.' But that was only part of the picture.

Lord Hailsham, in his book *The Case for Conservatism* (1947), put it like this:

Conservatives do not believe that political struggle is the most important thing in life. In this they differ from Communists, Socialists, Nazis, Fascists, Social Creditors, and most members of the British Labour Party. The simplest among them prefer fox hunting – the wisest religion ... The man who puts politics first is not fit to be called a civilised being let alone a Christian.

That is one among many views from politicians. The difference from the stone-throwing curate of Bethnal Green could not be more marked. But the Christian church – more specifically the Church of England – embraces them both; it is certainly a broad church.

Central to the position of the established church is that the Church of England is governed by Parliament. In 1927 the revised Prayer Book was brought to Parliament for ratification – the working party had been sitting since 1904, so some things don't change. The Lords voted it through but the Commons rejected it, even though it had clear majorities from the Church Convocations and Assembly. Those who are against change can deploy their lobbying power in the Commons to sustain opposition. Many of those will not be Christians but arguing from a broader view of concern for the wider fabric of society. This broader concern was evident in the debate on the ordination of women when the House of Commons voted over-whelmingly for change.

Shades of this argument were seen again in 1965 when those wishing to protect the Book of Common Prayer produced many establishment figures to argue for the purity of the historical writing. (We don't water down Shakespeare and people still understand him!) But the church had learnt a thing or two since the 1920s and the Act went through under the title of 'Prayer Book (Alternative and other Services) Measure'. Thirty years later some newcomers to the church can still be heard saying, 'But what is it the alternative to?' And when that is explained, exclaiming, 'But it's not the alternative. It's the norm.'

The upper reaches of the Church of England are very involved with the Privy Council, whose role is not widely understood. When the Normans invaded England they brought with them a strong idea of 'kingship'. This did not go down well with the Saxons who had strongly developed views on local government. So the King travelled around the country persuading the Saxons of the benefit of having a national King. The knights and courtiers who travelled with him, his friends who were close to him, who were privy to his views and who gave him counsel, became people of great influence. They were sought out by those wishing favours from the King.

The effectiveness of the Privy Council depended to a large extent on the strength of the King. When the King was weak, the Barons, who by the time of Henry III formed most of the Council, gained real power. From this body Parliament developed, and the Cabinet are still bound together by the Privy Council Oath of Secrecy. Leaders of opposition parties are appointed to the Privy Council so that under that Oath of Secrecy they can be told things by the Prime Minister in the national interest – which they can't then raise either in the House or with members of their own parties. A Privy Counsellor is for life, so they often head up government enquiries or Royal Commissions – as members of the great and the good.

The Archbishop of Canterbury is always the leading non-Royal Counsellor and the Archbishop of York is also a member. The only other bishop who is a member at the time of writing is the Bishop of London. But, once they retire, they remain Privy Counsellors, with the right to put the prefix 'Right Honourable' in front of their names. They have the right of access to the Monarch and, of course, are often called upon under the terms of the Privy Council Oath to give advice both formally and informally.

It is in the legal affairs of the church where it can be seen how close is the link between the established church and the state, and how complicated it would be, and how much parliamentary time it would take – and how rich some lawyers would get in the process – to separate the two! The Court of Arches is the chief court of the Archbishop of Canterbury. It was originally held in the parish church of St Mary-Le-Bow, in Cheapside, London, and then moved to the Hall of Advocates when St Mary-Le-Bow was destroyed in the great fire. This court originally dealt with a whole range of civil disputes which gradually came to be considered as not wholly or even necessarily ecclesiastical. For instance, its jurisdiction in matrimonial and testamentary matters was transferred in 1857 to the new Divorce and Probate Courts. Under the Court of Arches there are still held, from time to time, ecclesiastical courts in the various dioceses under the direction of a judge who becomes known as a Chancellor. They mostly deal with petitions for material or fabric alterations to churches. But they can, at very great expense, become involved in litigation between individual clergy and their bishop. The authority of these courts stems directly from the Privy Council, via the Archbishop of Canterbury and the Court of Arches. There is nothing remotely like this civil/ecclesiastical legal system in either the Roman Catholic, Methodist, or other Free Churches. There couldn't be – they are not established.

This is but one part of the interlocking jigsaw of church and nation. Jigsaw is an appropriate word. Both the constituency structure of the country and the English parish system mean that wherever an individual lives in the UK (even in Wales under the Church in Wales, or Scotland under the Presbyterian Church of Scotland) they are part both of a constituency and of a parish. Very much in the same way that the Labour member for Basildon is MP for all her constituents, whether or not they voted for her, so the Rector of Beckenham is rector for everyone living in his parish, whether or not they go to church. The parishes, even where there are team ministries or group parishes, have a great historical tradition. Populations move around so the church groups parishes under clergy where necessary, but the names of the parishes stay. In politics the boundary commissioners change the constituencies to try to keep a franchise of around 100,000 voters, compatible with size. You couldn't do it in the west of Scotland! The changes result in new constituencies springing up needing new names – often names with no historical or geographical background. That is a great loss of tradition, but it doesn't offend towns who otherwise might object to being put under the name of larger neighbours.

While there is much in common between priest and politician there is one area where there is no overlap. Priests, like lunatics, are barred from standing for the House of Commons. The antecedents for this date back to the time when there were three Houses of Parliament – the Lords, the Commons and the Clergy (House of Convocation). In 1295 Edward I called a special parliament of the clergy. The clergy claimed a right to vote their own taxation (tithes), payable until 1920, and refused to sit in a parliament with the laity on the grounds that this would involve them in taxation levied by a parliament summoned on a temporal basis. Thus their existence as a separate part of the constitution – sometimes called the third estate – was recognized. Because this pre-dated the Reformation this rule also applies to Roman Catholic priests. However, when Parliament was reduced to two Houses, the Lords and the Commons, bishops could be summoned to the House of Lords, because the Lords had no authority to impose taxation. In the nineteenth century an Act was passed allowing the clergy to give up their Holy Orders; if they did that they could stand for the Commons.

There can, however, be an anomaly, as happened in 1966. John Edmondson was ordained in the Church of England in 1958. The following year, his father, the First Baron Sandford, died and he inherited the title. Seven years later he was appointed to a ministerial position in the Conservative Government as Parliamentary Secretary at the Ministry of Housing. So, until the end of the twentieth century you could have a member of the clergy in the Government, but only if they were an hereditary peer!

Clergy who can't sit in Parliament can vote in all elections. By tradition, bishops, who lose their Lords' seats on retirement unless they are appointed Life Peers, don't (along with other peers) vote in parliamentary elections. The logic for this is that they already have a seat in Parliament, and Robert Runcie caused something of a stir in the 1980s when he insisted to the Returning Officer that he wanted to cast a vote, and did so. Perhaps this was not significant, but in its small way it highlighted the intricate and complex relationship between church and state, and priest and politician.

3

The Power and Problems of Prayer

I ONCE chaired a church discussion group the day after *Songs of Praise* had been broadcast from St Margaret's Church, Westminster – the parish church of the two Houses of Parliament. (The incumbent of St Margaret's is always chaplain to the Speaker.) 'I saw Tony Blair, next to Ann Widdecombe, next to Simon Hughes,' said one participant in amazement. 'And Ian Paisley, he wasn't there. But he's meant to be a Christian, isn't he? How on earth can they all do that. I know they take their religion seriously. I've read about Tony's problems attending Catholic mass with his wife. I know Ann Widdecombe became a Roman Catholic after the Church of England admitted women; and Pam Rhodes introduced Simon Hughes as Chairman of the all-party backbench committee on Christianity.' He was genuinely puzzled, as were other members of the group, and as is a wider audience. First, there is surprise that so many MPs, of whom all opinion polls show the public has a very low estimation, are devoted, and serious, Christians. Second, the question is asked, if Tony Blair, a Labour Prime Minister, Ann Widdecombe, a Conservative front-bench spokesperson, and Simon Hughes, a leading Liberal Democrat, can all broadly agree about what to them is obviously the most important factor in their lives – a belief in God and the hope of the resurrection – why can't they agree on the future of Europe, the National Health Service, and overseas aid? Third, why do they disagree with such bad manners and lack of courtesy, and behave in a way they would never dream of doing in the General Synod, in which some of them, like John Gummer, sat?

These are good questions and serve to underline the comparison between church and politics; and the confusion between unity and disagreement. The questions start from the false premise that the corporate church is generally united but has disagreements of various sizes on different scales, and the political parties are not united and that there are enormous differences between them.

In fact, in my experience, all political parties (no matter how misguided others may think) are united in their aim to achieve what they consider to be the common good. There are, at the end of the twentieth century, few points of philosophic principle between them. The Labour Party is no longer the party of nationalization; the Conservative Party no longer the party of Empire. On the big issues of our time – Northern Ireland, the political situation in the Balkans – there is cross-party consensus. On policies for the economy, education, fighting crime, it is now very much the case of each party slagging the other one off and saying in effect, 'We will do the same thing only better and more efficiently.' The differences are high-lighted, even when they are slight, in an effort to win votes and gain power.

The church has to win hearts and minds, but it doesn't have to win elections. All churches both think and feel that the one thing they should strive to offer their potential audience, which in theory is the whole of creation, is unity. They feel guilty that after 2000 years unity cannot be offered truthfully and wholeheartedly. So there is an (often unspoken and sometimes even unconscious) attitude of hiding disagreements and concentrating on those things that all the churches, and all strands of Christianity, even all religions, have in common.

The problem with this approach is that sometimes the world is offered the lowest common denominator and where the policy is successful real differences are pushed so far below current thought and activity that they are not explored. Yet, I remember Lancelot Fleming, then Bishop of Portsmouth and later to become Queen's Chaplain at Windsor, in the 1950s, urging on a conference of sixth-formers to 'Argue; discuss; debate; disagree. God gave you the gift of thinking and expressing yourself. Use it. Show the world that Christians not only have faith but think about their faith – even disagree about their faith.'

Fleming said this in the context of leading a session on the subject of both the power and the problems of prayer. Later, when he became a Life Peer and a member of the House of Lords he said that he wished members of the church, both clergy and laity, would have the same confidence as politicians to air their differences openly. 'Then perhaps the church would seem to people not just a place of peace and sanctuary but an exciting living part of God's will.'

It is perhaps in the area of prayer that there are more hidden differences of opinion than in any other area of the church. Half a century ago Fleming encouraged young people to express their views thus.

> You can read all the books ever written about prayer. You can study theology to Ph.D. level. You can preach as a Bishop on the subject. It may be different for everybody; there may be common threads. Some may be able to learn from others. But nobody knows. It is not a matter of intelligence, though it can be. Your views are as valid as mine.

The political comparison with the unwritten constitution is also valid. These are not things written in black and white, let alone tablets of stone. Each person's views are valid. The difference between views is great and sincere and deserves respect and consideration. Nobody would write about prayer unless they felt deeply about it and thought that they had something to offer which was different from the views of others, and from which others could gain.

Consider the differences in their views on prayer as expressed by these Christians of the twentieth century:

> To be with God for a space. Within this may be included every aspect of prayer which the textbooks have described. To be with God wondering, that is adoration. To be with God gratefully, that is thanksgiving. To be with God ashamed, that is contrition. To be with God with others on the heart, that is intercession. The secret is the quest of God's presence.
> (Michael Ramsey (Archbishop of Canterbury), *Be Still and Know*, 1982)

> Anyone who lives, prays. Anyone who possesses human life possesses a deeper spiritual life as well, and the journey of prayer is nothing more nor less than the gradual awakening to the reality of recognizing what is already there.
> (Delia Smith (cookery expert and writer), *A Journey into God*, 1998)

> Waiting is not an optional extra to the life of prayer, it is at its heart.
> (Richard Harries (Bishop of Oxford), *Turning to Prayer*, 1978)

> I pray for the people that they may not be able to sleep at night because of the man in the cardboard box.
> (Jackie Pullinger, a musician, as quoted by broadcaster and writer Libby Purves in her book, *Holy Smoke – Religion and Roots: A Personal Memoir*, 1998)

Here are four very different ways of approaching prayer. They represent different emphases along the spectrum of approach, from the desire to be utterly alone and undistracted and in the silence get the relationship with God right, to the feeling that God is everywhere in the world and that prayers don't necessarily need words, just a deep concentration of being because the creation is God's and he must therefore be in all of it.

These are all good people in any sense of the word, whose writings and broadcasts show that they have a profound sense of prayerful activity. Yet, contrast this with John Robinson's famous writings in *Honest to God*, first published in 1963 when he was Bishop of Woolwich:

> I believe the experts have induced in us a deep inferiority complex. They tell us that this is the way we ought to pray, and yet we find that we can not maintain ourselves for any length of time even on the lowest rungs of the ladder, let alone climb it. If this is the *scala sacra*, then it seems it is not for us. We are evidently not 'the type'. And so we carry on with an unacknowledged sense of failure and guilt.
>
> I can testify to this most strongly from the time I spent in a theological college, both as a student and as a teacher. Here was a laboratory for prayer. Here one ought to be able to pray, if one ever could. For here were all the conditions laid on – time, space, quiet ... I discovered there what I can only describe as a freemasonry of silent, profoundly discouraged, underground opposition, which felt that all that was said and written about prayer was doubtless unexceptionable but simply did not speak to 'our' condition.

The impact of this book was tremendous. It is one of the most talked-about books of the twentieth century. It put religious writing into the headlines, Parliament, and into the popular domain in a way no other book of recent times has done. Christianity was talked about. The braver clergy organized church debates on the issues it raised. This was the 'church' effective in the 1960s. These were also Robinson's words:

> I suspect we have got to ask very seriously whether we should even begin our thinking about prayer in terms of the times we 'set aside', whether prayer is primarily something we do in the 'spaces', in the moments of disengagement from the world. I wonder whether Christian prayer, prayer in the light of the Incarnation, is not to be defined in terms of penetration through the world to God rather than the withdrawal from the world to God.

Was this the spirit of God moving through the 1960s directly into his own church? For many it felt like it.

The notion that perhaps the best starting point for the power of prayer may not be withdrawal from the normal world in an attempt to set aside a special time to be with God – because paradoxically by withdrawing from the world one is removing oneself from the activity of God – is central to the modern debate about prayer. It raises two major questions: What is the point of prayer? What is the difference, if any, between prayer and what can be termed 'prayerful activity'?

All manner of experience suggests that prayer can be regarded as one of the most natural and primitive of instincts. Yet the exponents of prayer have to answer two criticisms. The first is theological: God does not need to be told the desires of humans. The second is scientific: the universe is governed by laws which could not be violated by the power of, or the answer to, prayers. Throughout history men and women have dealt with these questions in a variety of ways, without coming to any final answers. This recognition is essential to an understanding of the Christian view of prayer. It revolves around another central paradox: Christians are humans. Christianity is dependent on faith, but because we are human, no matter how strongly we believe in our interpretation of God's will, we could be wrong. Throughout the Christian centuries this thought has been stressed by preachers. Only 200 days before the end of the twentieth century I heard Steffan Conway, a clergyman in the Diocese of Rochester, say in a sermon, 'Always beware of the Christians who are absolutely certain they have the right answers, they are playing at being God.'

Even if prayer, like all matters pertaining to faith, is more about searching for the right questions rather than accepting (in limited human terms) answers, there is still a broad range of experience of prayer. I recognize that 'experience' is a dangerous concept here. For over thirty years I have been involved in the Church of England and one of the areas in which I have worked is in intercession – public prayer. A concern for public prayer must grow out of private prayer. Nevertheless this has meant that for 30 years I have been part of a changing group of those offering intercessions from my parish church. I have discussed prayers with the clergy and laity of that fellowship and I have attended and organized retreats and conferences at different levels in the Church of England, as well as trying to read and study widely and have discussions with believers and non-believers, both formally and informally. I have also, of course, in my terms, both thought and prayed (formally and informally!) about the subject. I offer that as my experience, aware of the fact that it must be considered in the light of the experience of others, and that it is very likely to consist of my own prejudices, boosted by selective judgements. I well remember overhearing a heated argument, from my days as a teacher, between a head and a deputy head. The headmaster was laying down the law, saying, 'I must be right. After all, I have had 25 years' experience.' His deputy, who was rather better at keeping her temper, smiled sweetly and said, 'Oh, no. What you really mean is that you have had one year's experience repeated twenty-five times.'

Always beware of the views of an expert. The classic definition was given by Prime Minister Harold Macmillan, in a speech in the 1960s: 'Ex – someone who is past it. Spurt – a drip under pressure.'

Having given those health warnings, it does seem to me that there are four different types of private (as compared with public) prayer. The first is simply the 'I want' prayer. Please God, I want a new bike. Please God make Mummy better. Please God let me pass my exams. These are simple prayers which may be expressed with intense feeling or may be casual, almost flippant. Undoubtedly they grow from the confusion that *can* result from children's early thoughts on God. The biblical story is told to young children and God is shown as a father, or more politically correctly, a parental figure. Children look to their parents to supply their needs. What more natural than that God, Father to us all, becomes part of the extended family, to be asked for things out of the power of earthly parents to give. The problem is described by R. S. Lee, in his book *Your Growing Child and Religion*:

> Prayer is a risky topic ... made more difficult for the young child because he has not yet acquired the ability to draw a clear distinction between reality and fantasy. In his fantasies he can make anything come true simply by imagining it. Parents will get constant evidence of this power of fantasy in their children, normally in their play but sometimes spreading into other activities as well. If God has the power to make anything 'come true' he is not governed by the principle of reality which the child is gradually learning to apply in the real world. Prayer will then come to be classified in the realm of fantasy, a way of escape from the limitations that hard matter of fact imposes on us.

This is not to say that simple, 'I want' prayers aren't sometimes effective. Experience has shown that they sometimes are. What proof can't show is whether God has intervened supernaturally; whether the intensity of thought and power in the prayer has had an effect we are unable to understand; or whether the concentration of the mind on a particular focus of a prayer has resulted in the person offering the prayer arriving at a satisfactory conclusion. (If I take a paper-round I can save up and buy a bike.)

The traditional answer from the priest when prayers like these don't produce a result is a mix of either/or. God has heard our prayer but knows what is best for us and that isn't part of his plan. God has heard our prayer and has answered it in our best interests but in ways we don't yet understand.

Often this simple way of praying is with people for all their lives. Sometimes it can seem almost a superstition. Watch the way many sportsmen and women cross themselves before going onto the field of play. Nothing necessarily wrong in that. A friend of mine who used to cross himself before going out to bat, when challenged by a member of the opposing team for seeking heavenly help for victory, replied, 'No. My ability is a gift from God. I'm reminding myself that I owe it to Him to make best use of it.'

Sometimes this type of prayer descends into a bargain. How many of us have said words to the effect of, 'Dear God, please get me out of this mess and I'll never do it again. And, I'll always go to church on Sunday. And be nicer to people.'

The danger of this kind of prayer is that it can lead both to a lack of thought about the seriousness of prayer and to devalue the concept of prayer, a concept Christians are trying to bring to the rest of the world. I know some highly intelligent Christians who, because of their fear of flying, always say a prayer for safety on take-off. In no way do I mock, or make light of their fear. The words and the activity may well be of help to them. But what do they think God is actually doing in situations like this? Richard Harries, Bishop of Oxford, makes the point like this:

> If God continually intervened to prevent events taking their natural course the result would be an unpredictable world. You are going down some steps. An old lady who puts her foot down at the same time as yourself stumbles and is about to fall down. In order to save her, divine power reverses the normal pull of gravity. The old lady does not fall. But neither will your foot go down on the step either; it too is affected by the reversal of the usual gravitational effect. After a few minutes of hilarity this kind of world would become a nightmare. It would be impossible to rely on anything, impossible to predict anything. (From *Turning to Prayer*)

Harries also makes the point that among the complexities of pondering the 'I want' prayer, Christians should at least be able to agree that the factor of the mutuality of love between God and his people should be present. He quotes as a non-Christian prayer this one, offered by an eighteenth-century businessman and taken from F. E. Fisher's *Economics* (1957):

> Oh Lord, who knowst I have mine estates in the City of London, and likewise that I have lately purchased an Estate Fee Simple in the

County of Essex. I beseech thee to preserve the counties of Middlesex and Essex from fire and earthquake. And, as I have a mortgage in Hertfordshire, I beg thee likewise to have an eye of compassion on that county. For the rest thou mayest deal with them as thou art pleased.'

The second type of prayer is concerned with knowing that one wants something – more yearns for something – but knows not what. It is so well and so sadly summed up by newscaster James Mossman's suicide note, when he wrote: 'I can not stand it any longer. But I do not know what it is.' This is not a solely Christian or even religious phenomenon. I talked to some fifth-formers in a South London comprehensive recently. The title was 'Lateral Thinking and Politics' but we spread our wings during the discussion and were talking about individual aspirations and ambitions. One girl said: 'I feel like that line in the title song of *Friends* – always stuck in second gear. I know I want help from somewhere, but I don't know what help, or where from.' In this search the Christian will turn to God in prayer and seek help. The non-believer will often seek a different type of help. Star signs have become very big business. Even the respectable broadsheets publish their pages of astrological predictions. Mystic Meg is as recognizable as the Archbishop of Canterbury. Courses on self-awareness abound in adult education institutions. Corner-shop newsagents and local newspapers carry advertisements for tarot readings. Fortune-tellers are still popular attractions on seaside piers, and in some cities seances are making a comeback.

There is certainly a yearning. In some cases this yearning takes the form of a 'prayerful activity'. In the 1960s, transcendental meditation became a fashionable practice. Some Christians saw an overlap of usefulness in such things as yoga. It was not just a question, as G. K. Chesterton would have us famously believe, of people when they don't believe in God believing in anything, but for many a genuine search based on all they had as a foundation – their own experience. John Robinson had anticipated this. In *The New Reformation* he wrote:

> Doctrine is the definition of experience; the revelation discloses itself as the depth and meaning of the relationship. To ask men to believe in the doctrine or to accept the revelation – before they see it for themselves – as the definition of their experience and the depth of their relationship, is to ask what to this generation, with its schooling in an empirical approach to everything, seems increasingly hollow.

This useful overlap between those who believe in God and seek his help and those who are seeking help through similar activity but without a Christian faith is well highlighted by *The Good Retreat Guide*, which side by side offers Christian, Buddhist, Hindu, Yoga and New Age retreat centres in Europe. It offers opportunities for silence, meditation and traditional prayer, but also for activities such as music, painting and gardening. This is very much a growth area with monasteries, convents, religious houses and other centres opening their doors to both groups and individuals for either private or organized retreats. They can be led or informal, and for the Christian the range of choice covers Anglican, Franciscan, Augustinian, Dominican, Benedictine, Black Spirituality, Pentecostalism and the Charismatic Movement. The Christian has a chance to learn from the Jesuits – either St Ignatius of Loyola, the founder, or the twentieth-century thinker Pierre Teilhard de Chardin; the spirituality of the sixteenth-century St Teresa of Avila; or Salesian spirituality; or the more recently developed interest in Celtic spirituality; or in any one of many strands of Christian thought. The range is impressive. But, just as the non-Christian is (normally) welcome to study these areas and experience the Christian conception of prayer, so the Christian is welcome to other centres where they may well learn from others lessons of value in their approach to prayer. For example, the Buddhapadipa Temple in Wimbledon has eleven monks in community who offer courses in study and meditation, including 'walking meditation', which might be just the thing for a busy person feeling guilty about not fitting prayer into a hectic day.

The third type of prayer is that which comes from a person who maintains that they are not asking anything for themselves, either general or specific, nor are they interceding for a third party; their prayer is to find out what God wants. This can set alarm bells ringing. Sometimes they think God tells them and then they tell the world. And the world is often very mistrustful. If you talk to God, that is prayer and it is acceptable. If you say you hear God's voice talking to you, telling you what to do – the criminal's defence (insane or not) throughout the ages – the danger is the world may think you mad. And the world may well be right.

People generally have more respect for (and take more notice of) those who are modest and reticent in telling us they have heard the will of God directly.

There is one section of the population for which this attitude is grossly unfair and for whom it poses problems: those who believe they have been genuinely called by God to the ministry and are then turned down by his selection committees on earth. For them, there are all kinds of difficult adjustments to be made. This has been especially apparent in the Church of England in recent years, amongst those women who were called by God but refused by man to proceed to the selection process. One woman deacon explained this to me at a retreat centre in Chislehurst where I was speaking to trainee clergy in the Rochester diocese. Complaining about the slowness of the church to respond to what she saw as God's will, she said: 'The Bishops fall over backwards to help those who disagree with women priests. Have these men any idea at all of the sheer pain, the spiritual slap in the face given to people like me.' She looked around her fellow deacons: 'I have been through university and training college with many in this room and now suddenly the establishment is saying to me – that's it. This is where you stop. It's not your spirituality, your intelligence, your compassion, your understanding, your capacity for hard work that we question. It's just your gender.' She then added: 'Because I feel God has a sense of humour I even prayed for a really outstanding priest to have a sex change – and see how the church got out of that!'

I found that it was because those women denied their calling had a sense of humour that they managed to cope. Instead of the bitterness – though there was some, in particular and understandably from some of the older women – there was grace. 'We didn't tell the men, that would have been rude,' said one deacon, 'but we laughed with Christ about the dear old funny Church of England.'

It seems to me that the fourth type of prayer is that which does not seek. It is not asking. It is just the person concerned wanting to be in the presence of God. This is often the stance of the really humble who are saying we don't know, or can't find the words; we just want to be with you. In your presence. Maybe we find your presence in the garden, or in music. Maybe we find your presence in a building, or a painting. Maybe we find your presence in recognizing the presence of Christ in one another. As Archbishop Ramsey said, there are many textbooks – but there are no rules.

Delia Smith summed it up in *A Journey into God*:

> God is not to be found in human wisdom and learning, nor by people with special privileges of intuition and understanding, nor yet through self-contrived transcendentalism (as some modern cults prescribe). Perhaps what distinguishes the Jewish and Christian traditions from others is that they are firmly rooted in the earth – 'the earth is crammed with heaven' – and in the commonplace of daily life. The

closer a person comes to God the more he is seen in the 'normality of day to day existence ... Prayer is life. 'Anyone who follows me will have the light of life as his guide' (John 8:12). Whoever is committed to prayer knows that the way to God is through everyday life. It is prayer that opens our spiritual eyes and ears to see and hear Him more clearly in all that we do.

In spite of the problems, that is the power of prayer.

4

Public Prayer

IN the Church of England it is on the axis of public prayer that Christianity and politics meet: often in accord; sometimes in inspiration; occasionally with conflict; but always hiding questions that are rarely raised. Because public prayer is not just the Church of England on parade with a collective voice: it also embraces the national psyche; can hold the nation together; and at a local and domestic level expresses in public thoughts of joy and respect appropriate to births, marriages and deaths.

Many people who are entirely comfortable with private prayer find the concept of public prayer difficult. To start with, it seems to presuppose that all those involved believe in God. If we bring before God non-believers does this not insult both the integrity of God and the person involved? If we argue that this is primarily a way of combining the country in grace, is that not a blatant misuse of Christ's sacrifice? Or, perhaps worst of all, if we say, 'It doesn't really matter, does it? There are far more important, pressing, relevant matters to worry about.' Doesn't this suggest we have lost our way as a Christian country?

One of the hidden questions that is rarely raised – and when it is, it is dismissed as either marginal or, paradoxically, too difficult to cope with – is to suppose that if the Monarch doesn't believe in God, does the whole structure collapse? And if a Monarch doesn't believe in God, is it 'better' in the sense of honesty and integrity for the Sovereign to say so and have a debate about abdication, or to carry on living a lie for the sake of the nation's good? Can goodness be achieved in that way?

The importance of this rarely heard question is that the establishment of the Church of England as the official national church is dependent on the position of the Queen as Head of State being

Defender of the Faith and Supreme Governor of the Church of England. At the moment we are inspired by the rock-solid integrity of a Christian Queen. The Prince of Wales has said he would rather be Defender of All the Faiths, and certainly there have been, during the 1990s, private, unofficial meetings held with bishops in Sheffield to discuss whether other faiths should make contributions to the next coronation.

This is significant. The most important public prayer, from which the authority for all other public prayers in the established church comes, is at the coronation. This thousand-year-old service is adjusted slightly for each monarch, but since the Reformation has been explicitly Protestant. In 1953 the Queen prayed in her coronation oath, 'To maintain in the United Kingdom the Protestant Reformed Religion established by law'. If we keep an established church in the UK the solemnity and indeed awe of that prayer must be seriously stressed in any public debate. Especially at a time when so many other changes in our constitutional life – devolution; reform of parliament; European legislation – are happening quickly and, to many people, suddenly.

The coronation dates from 973 when the Archbishop of Canterbury crowned King Edgar at Bath, when the King was called on to protect and serve the Church. The Monarch is flanked by the Bishop of Bath and Wells, for the South of England, and the Bishop of Durham, for the North. The Archbishop asks: 'Will you to the utmost of your power maintain and preserve inviolably the settlement of the Church of England? Will you preserve unto the Bishops and Clergy of England and to the Churches there committed to their charge, all such rights and privileges, as by law do or shall appertain to them?' If, at some time in the future, the answer to that question is going to be along the lines of, 'Well, yes, certainly. But not exclusively. Some of the rights and privileges will be changed to include others' then – whether or not in the words of *1066 and All That* that would be a good thing – we need a public debate.

It is not just at coronations that the Church of England gives authority and blessing to great state occasions. The prayers at weddings and funerals have, in the past, helped bring a cohesive quality to the life of the nation. To many people it is a way under the grace of God of bringing together (for instance) the very human characteristics of individuals and the awful majesty of death. Many found moving the prayers for Diana, Princess of Wales, offered by the Archbishop of Canterbury at her funeral in 1997:

We give thanks for qualities and strengths that endeared her to us; for her vulnerability; for her radiant and vibrant personality; for her ability to communicate warmth and compassion; for her ringing laugh; and above all for her ability to identify with those less fortunate in our nation and the world.

There was debate about the inclusion of Elton John's song 'Goodbye England's rose'. Many were moved by the song's words. But how fantastic: a debate in the 1990s about what constituted a prayer! When was the last time that happened?

Prayers for the royal family have spotlighted the fact that, like private prayers, their point is all about asking questions rather than seeking certain answers. In the 1920s there was a serious academic survey done to see if all the prayers offered by all the churches every Sunday meant that the members of the royal family lived longer than other upper-middle-class people. It concluded that they didn't, so asked what was the point of the prayers. A few months ago, one commentator said that their high-profile lifestyles had made their family lives more vulnerable than most, and that was why they needed our prayers!

Specific prayers for the nation are held in churches of all denominations at times of national rejoicing or celebration. Often particular towns hold Civic Sundays with prayers for the Mayor, councillors and local organizations. Mayors, together with, where appropriate, High Sheriffs and Lord Lieutenants, as representatives of the Queen (the Defender of the Faith), have a duty to attend such events irrespective of their beliefs, but not, interestingly, Members of Parliament.

MPs have absolutely no constitutional role in their own constituencies other than representing the place at Westminster. If you glimpse an MP tucked in next to local civic dignitaries in the front row of the pews he or she is there not by right but by invitation. If the prospective candidates from other political parties have any sense (let alone any belief) they will be there too.

The one civic occasion which causes some priests and other church members to feel uneasy is Remembrance Sunday. With few serving priests having been involved in the Second World War, and not many still practising who did national service, this is perhaps understandable. Sometimes part of the church puts up the Aunt Sally of not wanting to glorify war. This really is a nonsense. I, in common I suspect with many, have met very few people – certainly not those with direct experience – who wish to glorify war. Reconciliation and forgiveness can be a more difficult problem, but that is a separate issue.

Curiously, the one service outside the Christian canon of Christmas, Easter and Pentecost with which the church seems entirely happy is that of Harvest, an Old Testament festival (see Leviticus and Deuteronomy). Giving thanks for harvest to whatever gods are suitable obviously pre-dates Christianity by thousands of years. Yet the church embraces this festival easily with joyful words and music. This is a celebration of immemorial antiquity and worldwide distribution; it seems to have played little part in the life of Christ, and is largely ignored by theologians. It is not a big national event: television does not flit from services at St Pauls to farms around the country and the hedgeless arable tracts of East Anglia. But at parish level it is big, with masses of opportunity for children to make, colour and perform, and a chance for clergy to preach on relevance in our changing world as they direct tins of kiwi fruit to local homes for the elderly.

Otherwise, most public prayer is based around the circle of the Christian year. Some, especially newcomers without the tradition of a Christian education, find this difficult. 'You never seem to get anywhere,' one young man said to me after coming to church for a few months. 'You just go round and round in circles, looking backwards all the time.' He was a market researcher: 'You have your average attender for about 70 hours of the year and for at least 50 you are looking backwards.'

Conversely, many churchgoers find both comfort and inspiration in the stability of following the church year and knowing the forms of the liturgy, the words of the hymns, and the continuity of the prayers. That is why there is always opposition when new measures are suggested or introduced.

This opposition must be taken seriously and with respect. It often comes from the elderly who feel that they are being undermined when they see the forms of worship in which they grew up changing for reasons they think are not valid. All of us in the church are not always all that good in explaining change.

One problem is this: change in the Church of England is, generally speaking, handed down from above after some kind of working party has reported back to the General Synod. On the whole it doesn't flow up from the pews. Yet, at one grass-roots level, change is happening locally: where churches of different denominations in one area are learning to work together in worship and witness. It has proved impossible for a blueprint to be worked out on high and handed down to the parishes. Some parishes, having done some extremely successful work in this way, are now feeling a measure of discontent that they can't be more effective as a base focal point for change in their own churches.

The controversy about prayers offered in church services is a case in point. All clergy will tell you of the difficulties – to a greater or lesser degree – that they have with their congregations. One summed it up like this:

> We have to use words. You can't just ask people to sit in silence and hope for collective praying. I know it sounds a politically correct cliché, but words must be relevant. Safety from dangers on the road should command our prayers much more in the 1990s than the 'perils of the night' and when I try to explain that I get someone complaining that if it is so important to have up-to-date language for prayers why is it not important to have up-to-date dress for the clergy. Why should one historical tradition stay and one go? I simply say the Church can only do one thing at a time – and then they say that they don't want the dress updated!

When the Church of England decided to revise the order of service, and the prayers used in services in the 1970s, they avoided the debacle of the 1920s by introducing suggested changes in a series of offerings to be tried out as monitored experiments in selected churches. Scope was given for the Book of Common Prayer to continue to be used, but irrespective of the Church of England's view as to its appropriateness for modern worship; it was accepted by both church and state that the book was a national English legacy and an important part of both our religious and literary heritage.

The Book of Common Prayer is in one sense a product of the Reformation, since it originated from the demand that the public worship of the church should be conducted in English. But the materials from which it is compiled are the services of the medieval church, which themselves developed from the rites of the early Christian centuries. To this must be added the influence of the Reformation's Orders of Public Worship which are attributed to Archbishop Herman in 1543.

The first authorized service in English was the Litany, translated and adopted by Archbishop Cranmer, approved by the House of Convocation, and enforced by Parliament in 1549 by the first Act of Uniformity. The reforming language of Ridley and Hooper led to a second Prayer Book in 1552 and there was another revision on the accession of Elizabeth I in 1559. Prohibited during the days of

Cromwell's Commonwealth, it became once more the 'Service Book of the Nation' at the Restoration. Since 1662 there has been no major revision. In the early part of the twentieth century Parliament, by means of Royal Letters to the convocations of Canterbury and York, instructed a process to begin to enquire into the advisability of another revision. After 25 years, a report was presented to Parliament which was finally rejected by the House of Commons. The 'Book of Common Worship (year) 2000' suffered no such problem. Based on the radical measures of previous years there was no need to re-fight battles. The war had been won.

When, in the 1970s, the Church of England introduced its then new measures, it was at pains to point out: 'The Alternative Service Book, as its name implies, is intended to supplement the Book of Common Prayer, not to supersede it.' The official line was that, 'The Church's worship is a continuous process, and that any liturgy, no matter how timeless its qualities, also belongs to a particular period and culture' (ASB Preface). Well, that may well have been the expressed intention. It may well have been the real intention, but it hasn't turned out like that. You would be hard put to find more than a handful of churches where the Alternative Service Book hasn't superseded the Book of Common Prayer at regular Sunday worship.

As if in anticipation of this, there is a preamble to the Alternative Service Book which puts the Church of England's view on the necessity for change. That in itself is a remarkable situation: the growing realization that public relations demands an established church explains its conduct to its members. The preamble reads:

> It is a remarkable fact that for over three hundred years and despite all attempts at revision, the Book of Common Prayer has remained the acknowledged norm for public worship in the Church of England, as well as the model and inspiration for worship throughout most of the Anglican Communion.
>
> Rapid social and intellectual changes, however, together with a world wide re-awakening of interest in liturgy, have made it desirable that new understandings of worship should find expression in new forms and styles. Christians have become readier to accept that, even within a single church, unity need no longer be seen to entail strict uniformity of practice. The provision of alternative services is to be seen as an enrichment of the Church's life rather than a threat to its integrity ... The gospel of the living Christ is too rich in content, and the spiritual needs of his people are too diverse, for a single form of worship to suffice.

The church took enormous trouble to get this book on the statute. Parliament was assured that the Prayer Book (Alternative and Other

Services) Measure 1965 was the result of the work of the Liturgical Commission set up ten years earlier. MPs were informed that every part of the book had been subject to detailed scrutiny by the General Synod – the governing body of the Church of England (largely or partly democratic, depending on your point of view) – and that the Synod understood the minds of the people in the pews. Once this measure had gone through – the Cabinet, and both Houses were told – there were no plans for any more changes in liturgical business. When measures of doctrine and worship were consolidated in 1974, the church made a point of publishing:

> The doctrine of the Church of England is grounded in the holy Scriptures, and in such teachings of the ancient Fathers and Councils of the Church as are agreeable to the said Scriptures. In particular such doctrine is to be found in the Thirty-nine Articles of Religion, the Book of Common Prayer and the Ordinal.

I talked about this to a Christian MP, Eric Heffer, on the terrace of the Commons one afternoon. He had just read the Bill. 'Ah,' he said, 'how very wise of them not to try and rewrite the Thirty-nine Articles!'

Of course, the Alternative Service Book came in for criticism. Thank God. It means people are thinking about their prayers and what they are saying. *Private Eye* especially had great fun with spoof services and the congregation's responses, in particular with their series casting Tony Blair as the vicar of St Albions. And I have now heard the story from four different members of the clergy of how they tapped the microphone and mistakenly said, 'There appears to be something wrong here', to get the full-throated chorus back, 'And also with you!'

The way in which most Christians are involved with public prayer is in their parishes each Sunday at intercessions which are now normally led by a member of the laity and where there is considerable scope for individual initiative. This is one of the ways in which the new services are offering people the opportunity to present to God their actual concerns and anxieties on behalf of their communities, as opposed to their perceived worries as laid down by church authorities. There is tremendous variety in this form of public prayer. I know of one church which presents with great decorum a slide show. Prayers for the local hospital are accompanied by photographs. Though the format differs, the structure is broadly the same. The words written in the service book offer intercessions for the church, the world, ourselves, those in trouble (including the sick), and for the commemoration of those who have died.

The public intercessions are either introduced by the incumbent, or directly started by the member of the congregation leading the prayers, in this way: 'In the power of the Spirit and in union with Christ, let us pray to the Father.' This is a change in the new 'Book of Common Worship' from the Alternative Service Book, which started: 'Let us pray for the Church and the world, and let us thank God for his goodness.' I can see that the substitution of the word 'Father', replacing 'God', may cause some problems with parts of feminist theology, and I wonder about the amount of thought that has gone into the 'power' of the Spirit, but the 'union' with Christ. As strong a case could be made for praying in 'union' with the Spirit and the real 'power' of Christ. But the Synod committee who compose these prayers did hope they would be used with flexibility, so there is scope for congregations to come to their own judgements on the suitability of which words they use – and in what order.

The next section goes: 'Almighty God, our heavenly Father, you promised through your Son Jesus Christ to hear us when we pray in faith.' William Marston, the Vicar of Crawley, took a group of us through these words in some detail and we concluded that reminding God of his promise was not the rudeness it first seemed. It is a way of reminding us of the responsibility we have in responding to the holy promise, before we start asking for anything.

The intercessions then move on to deal with the church: 'Strengthen N our bishop and all your Church in the service of Christ; that those who confess your name may be united in your truth, live together in your love, and reveal your glory in the world.' There is a point worth pondering about 'our' bishop and 'your' church and how it would feel if the pronouns were reversed. Many people, having prayed for their bishop will also want to pray for the clergy in their own church. This can raise problems of language. Some of the men like to be described as 'Father'; this may present difficulties if one of the clergy is a woman. 'Mother' is obviously not right; 'Sister' is 'downgrading' – the men would then have to be called 'Brother', which would lead to confusion with monks and nuns; simply to say 'Reverend' highlights the fact that there is a problem. Thus, some churches have solved this by dropping titles and using Christian names.

The prayers then go on to the world: 'Bless and guide Elizabeth our Queen; give wisdom to all in authority; and direct this and every nation in the ways of justice and of peace; that men may honour one another, and seek the common good.' Here I do offer some criticism, which I hope is done in a helpful spirit. (I am also interested in why in the previous paragraph we pray for the bishop to be 'strengthened' but here for the Queen to be 'guided'. I wonder what the reaction of the Almighty would be if we asked him to 'guide' the bishop, and 'strengthen' the Queen?)

It seems to me that this paragraph is out of date. First, looking around the world today, and especially the political world where there are many people who have a real control and sway over the lives of others, I see that they are not figures of authority. But they are very considerable figures of influence. Some are easily identifiable. No one would say that Tim Bell, or Chris Evans, or Posh Spice are figures of authority; but they do have an influence that affects the lives of other people. Some figures of influence – 'lurk in the shadows' is too dramatic a phrase – are not readily known, but their power over opinion-formers is very real. They need our prayers and should be included.

With the number of smaller wars growing around the globe since 1945, and four of them – Korea, the Falklands, the Gulf, and the Balkans – having affected the UK and thus calling into consideration the traditional church's criteria for waging a just war, it is obviously right to pray for peace. But with the concept of a just war presented to us by the church, we should also consider the price of peace. Is the sacrifice of honour worth paying for peace? Substitute the word 'pride' and I suspect most would say yes. But is tyranny or genocide a price worth paying for not fighting? These are areas where I think more hard thought is needed and perhaps peace used too casually.

Equally casual can be thoughts on the 'common' good. With under three minutes to offer intercessions, the congregation doesn't want a mini seminar on the fact that Christians will disagree on what makes up the 'common' good, let alone getting agreement on what is 'good', a question even Plato found complicated. This is one of the factors to consider if people supporting different political parties, with different views on the meaning of the 'common good', are to come together as Christians in the same broad-based church. But if thought is not given to what motivates the genuine differences in the area of the 'common good', it is easily possible to pray publicly and include the congregation in intercessions to which some are profoundly opposed. On the other hand, to try to avoid that situation can result in the kind of wishy-washy prayers that can give Christian polemic a bad name. 'What do we want?' – 'Moderate reform.' 'When do we want it?' – 'In due course.' This section of our public prayers needs more attention.

'Give grace to us, our families and friends, and to all our neighbours; that we may serve Christ in one another, and love as he loves us.' Grace is a marvellous word. Difficult to define but instantly recognizable. It is a word like 'love' which can be used as both a verb and a noun and one which perhaps more than most conveys the image of God's Holy Spirit moving among us. The workings of the Holy Spirit are not mentioned directly in these prayers. Years ago the Church became worried that the mention of the Holy Ghost (as it was then called) might send out all kinds of wrong signals to confused or vulnerable people; that visions of the Holy Ghost might become mixed up with clanking chains and screams in the night. Although the church does have a policy on ghosts and exorcism, some clergy find it difficult to present it to the general public from within the same organization that seeks to provide practical aid for the relief of poverty. Yet, as one sixth-former said to me, 'I feel no sense of personal involvement with Jesus. Thinking about a loving God is just too difficult to cope with at the same time as the Balkan refugees need help, but I do actually see some kind of spirit moving around bringing out kindness in people.' She went on, 'It is almost as though God is stepping aside from the Balkans but the Holy Spirit is working like mad among us to bring out the best in humanity. Unfortunately I think he is losing, but at least he is trying.'

What is empirically true is that it is possible to observe communication between people which is not direct, such as for instance (as happened to me), the combined feeling of awe, experienced by a small party of visitors to the crypt of the Basilica of the Nativity in Manger Square, Bethlehem, the supposed site of the birth of Christ. No one said anything, but afterwards we soon established that there was a collective, common feeling. There is strong evidence for suggesting that the Holy Spirit, often in the form of grace, is moving in the collective unconscious.

From praying for families and friends, the intercessions move on to a more outward look, for those without families and friends, the lonely and the sick: 'Comfort and heal all those who suffer in body, mind, or spirit ...; give them courage and hope in their troubles; and bring them the joy of your salvation.' The dots are where members of individual churches are encouraged to announce the names of those for whom they have been specifically asked to pray.

At one level this is an extremely useful tribal noticeboard. 'Good Heavens, I didn't know poor old Peggy was back in hospital. I wonder who is looking after her cats. I must do something about it.' That kind of thing. Though there are deeper thoughts here. 'Heal all those who suffer in body' does not mean praying for all those who are ill to recover. If we prayed in that manner, and God answered our prayers, no one would ever die and so no one would ever find the salvation of God. Frank Fisher, then Chaplain of Goldsmiths College, once told the audience at a Rotary lunch: 'The great thing about dying is that it is the only aspect of life where you don't have to say "I don't think I'll be able to do that!"' I saw the point put well in St Faith's Church in Lee-on-Solent, Hampshire. The Vicar (or Padre, as many in this naval village still called him) had rigged up a movie screen and showed an extract from a film (called, I think, *The Invasion of the Killer Tomatoes from Outer Space*). Discussing Earth, one alien is saying to another, 'Don't ever go there. I've been watching that place. No one gets out alive.'

Healing is much more about making whole, a process which Christians believe takes place each side of the event of dying. It is a most moving, humbling and inspiring experience to speak with someone who knows they are near death, and yet are very clearly a 'pretty whole person', as was said about the actor John Le Mesurier whose – planned – last words were, 'It's all been a lot of fun really', and who had arranged a note to go into the personal columns of *The Times* the day after he died telling his friends how much he would miss them.

We must also be careful in giving public prayers of thanks for those who have recovered from illness or operation. Too much public celebration will be bound to raise in the minds of those whose relatives and friends have not recovered: 'Why them – why me?'

I also feel that perhaps this is an area where to the non-Christian world we may seem to be putting too much pressure on God and not enough on ourselves. Here the laity can learn much from politicians. (Not, I think, the clergy. It seems in the 1990s that those who wish to be involved in action as well as words are doing so, perhaps not in the most effective way, but we shall come to that.) The laity doing the intercessions ask God to help the sick: they should ask God to show them what we can do to help.

A shorthand view of creation is that God gave man and woman free will, and we messed up his world by exercising that free will in a selfish way. But God also gave us the gifts of intelligence, organization, compassion, the capacity for hard work. We should pray for help in directing those talents towards those who suffer. If that means not just asking God to bring them 'the joy of your salvation' each Sunday, but getting out and involved in the real world with the problems of health and education, so be it.

'Hear us as we remember those who have died in the faith of Christ
...; according to your promises, grant us with them a share in your
eternal kingdom.' I heard this next section of prayers severely
criticized at a retreat/conference I attended. A woman there said,
with some force, 'It's not those who died in the faith of Christ that
need our prayers. They will be looked after. It's all those poor souls
who died outside the faith that need to be prayed for.' This provoked
quite an argument. Someone maintained that those who died outside
the faith should be divided into two groups: those who had never
heard of Christ and had had no opportunity to be received into the
church, including those misguided people of other beliefs who had
been fooled into thinking that there were other ways of salvation than
through Christ; and those who had every opportunity to come to
Christ, through education, discussion, thought and access, and were
entirely able to make up their own minds but had rejected
Christianity – it was insulting to their memory and their integrity to
offer prayers knowing they wouldn't have wanted them when alive.
This produced a remark which I think in many ways sums up the
Christian dilemma (if dilemma it is) of modern times. One elderly
man exploded: 'Oh no. There is only one way. Either you believe
salvation is only through Jesus Christ, or you don't. If you believe
that, you have a duty to bring as many people to Christ as possible –
whether they want to or not. If you don't believe that there is no
other way than Christ's, what on earth is the point of Christianity?
You might just as well say it's only about being very nice to everyone.'
The debate will continue.

The only other change that has been made from the words of
intercessions laid out in the Alternative Service Book is dropping 'all
Christian people' from the lines, 'Rejoicing in the fellowship of (N of)
and all your saints, we commend ourselves and all Christian people to
your unfailing love.' These words are replaced by 'the whole
creation'. This was in response to complaints from the parishes that
'all Christian people' was ending the prayers on an exclusive note,
rather like celebrating being in a private club, when what was needed
was to strike a much more outgoing note. This has now been done.

As the intercessions come to an end it is marvellous to dwell on the
word 'rejoicing', especially when uttered by someone who obviously
does rejoice. It lifts the spirits.

The last words of the intercessions offered by the Alternative
Service Book are 'Merciful Father,' (and then the congregation
joining in) 'accept these prayers for the sake of your Son, our Saviour
Jesus Christ. Amen.' I am always glad when I am doing the

intercessions and I get to the 'merciful' Father. It reminds me that no matter how badly I might have messed up the prayers, stumbled over key words, left out a name from the list of the sick, in fact, got it all wrong and upset some people in the congregation, hopefully a 'merciful' Father will understand and not worry too much. After all, he has millions of prayers coming through all the time; perhaps mine gave him a laugh.

Prayers pinpoint one of those areas of religious life where there can be too much emphasis on words of submission, and not enough on words leading to action. This is partly because many regard the pinnacle of prayer as being in silent communion with God, away from the bustle of the world. Some people look to the prayers offered in contemplative communities and try to work towards that model, recognizing that in those terms their prayers are going to be many steps down the ladder. There is a place for going to God and saying, 'This is me. These are my problems; please help.'

Public prayers are of a different order. We are praying for the church; for its organization to be effective in the world. We are praying for the determination of world events. We are bringing to the fore and to public attention the fact that the church cares about such things as poverty, war, housing, health, education. The important point is that as well as being Christians, we can also be effective citizens. Hopefully our Christianity has given us a responsibility towards others. The state has given us the machinery of Parliament and government. Nations have given us international organizations. In the UK we have a democracy in which we have both a vote and the opportunity to compete for media and political attention. The issues we offer to God in public prayer in our parishes are matters we have selected because they affect our world, our nation, our community and our parish. These are matters we care about. If we care about them enough to bring them before our God we surely care enough about them to use the gifts God has given us to be effective in whatever way is appropriate to us in engaging them directly in God's world.

This is where the church meets the state and the linchpin of effectiveness is in an understanding of the functions and organization of our system of government. The starting-point is Parliament.

5

Parliament: The Commons

IN the early part of 1999 I was talking with Jerry Hayes, the Conservative MP who lost his seat in the 1997 general election, and with a mutual friend of ours who was a clergyman. Jerry was saying to the clergyman, 'It's relatively easy starting out in your profession. You get the call. That tells you which part of the spectrum you are on from Free Church to Roman Catholic – or in the Church of England from high to low. You go to college; get ordained; become a curate; get priested; get a parish. You're on your way. But politics. Nowadays. Ugh.'

I knew what Jerry meant. Unlike members of the clergy, politicians are allowed, even encouraged, to be openly ambitious. They have views – like the clergy – and they want to put them into practice. They seek the places of power and influence – some point of access to Number 10, the Cabinet, Parliament. But which point? And how to get there? Having received the call to become a member of a political party – or, as does sometimes happen, having decided on a political career and made a calculation as to which party was going to be in power at the right time and then joined that – what next? No longer is it simply a case of finding a seat held by an MP of an opposing party, doing well there, and being rewarded with a safe seat yourself. Serious thought must be given to where real power will lie in the future. Should one's sights be set not on Westminster, but on the European Parliament, or the EU Commission, or regional assemblies, or becoming an elected town mayor, or even joining quangos and hoping for a seat in the new House of Lords? It is a minefield for career selection for a political hopeful, expressly counter-pointed after the 1997 general election, when the Labour Party's enormous majority meant that Parliament would – no matter what delaying tactics it used – merely be a rubber stamp for the Government.

The aspiring MP had to decide whether it was worth taking the chance, confident of being soon a member of the Government, or risk a life on the back benches, possibly doing great work for constituents but not being involved in the big problems of world peace or producing mass employment or saving the National Health Service, the realms of which they had dreamed.

This is a real problem for the twenty-first century. But, even if Parliament is at this time only acting as a rubber stamp for the executive, it is important to remember that the rubber stamp must be there. No matter what laws the executive wants to enforce on the people, the parliamentary process has to be gone through, and delay does give interest groups and individuals the opportunity to raise new ideas, point out dangers, and organize public debate. All this has to be done before the Queen in Council gives the Royal Assent to a bill and it becomes an Act of Parliament and law of the land. I am told an eight-year-old wrote, having listened to a lesson on the Queen: 'Oh, what a busy person she is. In the morning she defends the faith. In the afternoon she makes laws.' The Monarch is the cornerstone of church and state.

Throughout history the church has certainly given the Monarch an easier ride than the organizations of the state. The church has never beheaded its Supreme Governor and was always happier to live with the concept of the Divine Right than Parliament was. Indeed, ecclesiastics welcomed it.

For a time, the theory of the Divine Right of Kings ran in tandem with the doctrine of the Apostolic Succession. The mission given to the Apostles by Christ (John 20; Matthew 27) must extend to their legitimate successors in an unbroken line until the end of the world. The Roman Catholic interpretation is that the method of preserving the succession, and thereby preserving the Apostolic faith, is through the episcopate alone; the Apostles having laid their hands on their successors, who in turn ordained other bishops – the line of succession being thus maintained until the present day.

There were echoes of this in the theory of Divine Right which can still be heard and seen – especially with the anointing of oil from the ampulla at the coronation. The theory of Divine Right stated that all authority has a divine sanction and that the sovereign power does not exist merely by the will of the people or the consent of the government. The power of the Monarch comes from inheritance. This was the fundamental cause of the Civil War. The establishment of William and Mary on the throne in 1688 was a rude shock to the theory. The accession of the Hanoverian dynasty in 1714 with the title based on parliamentary Act of Settlement rendered the theory untenable. But inheritance is still the key factor in deciding who is our Head of State (as it therefore is in deciding who is Defender of our Faith). Until recent times all governments were reluctant to tamper with the fact of inheritance making up the major part of the House of Lords.

Parliament (like churches) has evolved. It is very much the child of its own history. Without an appreciation of that it is difficult either to understand the workings of Parliament or be effective in using its machinery. To those who say 'Why bother?', the answer is that the workings of Parliament touch our lives at many points. If we work, or don't work, we are subject to financial regulations and benefits decided by Parliament. When we drive our cars it is politicians who say how, where and when we can – by a variety of well over a thousand bye-laws, Orders in Council, and laws stemming from Acts of Parliament. Arrangements for births, marriages and deaths all come from parliamentary regulations. We may think we don't need politicians, but we have certainly got them; and they certainly won't go away.

Parliament today is dominated by the political parties. Without the active support of a political party it is impossible to win a seat at a general election. It is true Martin Bell won Tatton as an Independent in 1997, but he had the help and support of the Labour Party who did not put up a candidate to oppose him (by-elections are different matters).

This was not always the case. Until the nineteenth century many Independents sat in Parliament, grouping and regrouping with fellow MPs around different subjects. Until the Place Act in the eighteenth century many civil servants actually sat in Parliament, doing the jobs now done by junior ministers but serving successive administrations. There was not the same tense 'party' atmosphere. There was a tense atmosphere because members sat in a chamber designed like the crypt, where historically they first sat, facing each other across choir stalls. In theory this produces more bad-tempered clashes than is the case when members sit in a semi-circular chamber. To counteract this a coloured strip of carpet runs along the floor in front of both front benches. When MPs speak they must keep their feet firmly placed behind this line. It is so placed that if two MPs, one from each side, each draw their swords to attack the other, the swords won't quite meet (hence the saying, 'toeing the line'). Before any members of the Church of England snort and say how pathetic, just think: are you sure you haven't any historical customs in your own parish church which bear no relevance to today?

Party tension did not develop until the 1832 Universal Franchise Act created the need for structured political parties to get the vote out. Pocket and rotten boroughs disappeared and Conservatives and Liberals needed local organizations. Later the Labour Party needed formal local associations to select and support their candidates. All-embracing party organizations meant that when splits in policy developed they were harder to contain: the Corn Laws in the last century; the Irish question at the start of this century; Europe at the end of the century.

Parliament and its members are continually changing. One of the more significant ways in which it has changed this century is described by Harold Macmillan in his book *The Past Masters*:

> At that time (the 1930s) many Members had no desire at all for political advancement. On the Conservative side a large number, young and old, had come into the House of Commons as their fathers and grandfathers had done, from a general feeling that it was the right way to serve their country, and especially the localities in which they lived. It was quite remarkable how many constituencies, sometimes boroughs, more usually counties, had a long record of electing men of the same family, generation after generation. These were generally men of independent means as well as independent ideas.

The idea that these people would travel around the country as carpetbaggers looking for a seat away from their home area was quite foreign. Even in the 1950s and 1960s there were a great many who didn't want any job in government, merely (*sic*) to look after their constituents. One Conservative whip said to me that the Government couldn't have a three-line whip on a Monday as too many of their shire members would still be in their constituencies. He added that he couldn't ring up, say, Sir Walter Bromley-Davenport and tell him that if he didn't turn up to vote he may not be in the running to be considered for the job of Assistant Postmaster General. Not only did he know the kind of answer he would get, he would be the laughing stock of White's. There was a mirror image on the Labour benches. Ex coal-miners and trades union officials had come into Parliament as an extension of their jobs of looking after their members. Like the paternal members of the Conservative Party their first loyalty was not to government or party but to constituency.

How times have changed. Now, not only is it the case that all new MPs of the main parties want to get into government, the 'pay roll' vote has been increased by many more parliamentary private secretary appointments (paradoxically not paid but now considered – unlike in the 1960s – to be part of government) to accommodate them. Many would say this is entirely appropriate as unlike previous generations of MPs most have never had a job outside the political spectrum of lecturing, lobbying or researching.

Westminster is a Royal Palace. Even though the Monarch is not allowed in the chamber of the House of Commons – hence Black Rod and all the knocking on the doors of the Commons at the State Opening – she presides, in an unwritten constitutional way, over the Lord Great Chamberlain, which is an hereditary office originally granted to the De Vere family (the Earls of Oxford) but now alternating between three families. The current holder is the Marquess of Cholmondeley. Together with Madam Speaker and the Lord Chancellor, he is responsible for Westminster Hall, the Royal Apartments, the Robing Room, the Royal Gallery, and with the Earl Marshall – another hereditary post, held by the Duke of Norfolk – the arrangements for the State Opening of Parliament. (He should not be confused with the Lord Chamberlain – without the Great – who looks after the Royal Household and the Swan Warden, who is a professor, and the Barge Master. He used to have the job of censoring West End plays, but we have moved on.)

Some of the Doorkeepers of the Palace spend the mornings escorting parties around the building. In answer to the question, 'How many people actually work here?' they take great delight in replying, 'About half of them'. In fact, to see some of the 3500 who inhabit the place milling around in the course of a normal sixteen-hour working day would make a cynic wonder if much work is done at all – unless you count work as walking the seven miles of green (Commons) or red (Lords) carpets and standing around gossiping. For whips and parliamentary lobby correspondents gossiping is what a large part of the job entails.

The Palace of Westminster is just like a self-sustaining village on the banks of the Thames. To support the 659 MPs and 1078 peers (as at the end of 1999) who could attend, there is a vast army of secretaries, researchers, librarians, clerks, messengers, doorkeepers, police, caterers, bar staff, painters, carpenters, fabric restorers, bricklayers and hairdressers – even someone to look after the rifle range, another to check that all the pawns are in place in the chess room (there must be an analogy there somewhere), and yet another to make sure the snuff box is in its place on the ledge outside the Commons chamber for members wishing to take a sniff before entering. That is the legislators' support. Not necessarily to offer support are parliamentary lobby journalists and their staff, and lobbyists for vested interests who manage to get in under one guise or another. There is even the odd (well most are pretty odd) spook wandering around.

The Palace is unique both as a building and as an organization. It shares this with Westminster Abbey. The Abbey, officially the Collegiate Church of St Peter in Westminster, is a Royal Peculiar, and thus under the direct control of the Queen. ('What, the Palace and the Abbey?', our eight-year-old might say. 'What a busy Queen; however does she get out of Westminster?') It is all part of the intertwining of church and state; indeed for many years in the thirteenth century the House of Commons actually sat in the Abbey. Both buildings are historical monuments, and both international tourist attractions. Both are also working centres with varying degrees of authority, power and influence. There are powerful men and women in these buildings with ambitions for the nation and for their own futures, and these people stab each other in the back from time to time as people have throughout the Christian centuries.

At the heart of the Palace of Westminster is the chamber of the House of Commons. This is the one body that can authorize the Government to raise money by taxation to be used as Parliament, in theory, but the executive, in practice, chooses. It must be said though that at the end of the twentieth century the heart is pretty weak. Members don't go and activities in the chamber go largely unreported, apart from the official record kept by Hansard. There are reasons for this. Most of the serious business in the chamber is done on Tuesdays, Wednesdays and Thursdays in the afternoons. Cosmetic changes are made occasionally, with sometimes the House sitting on Wednesday mornings. Fridays is given over to private members' business and Monday sees MPs returning from their constituencies. During the first part of each afternoon, for an hour from 2.30 p.m. onwards, questions are asked of specific ministers: education, agriculture and so on. Questions to the Prime Minister now occupy half an hour from 3 p.m. each Wednesday. Questions fall into three types: to try to find out information; to make a point; to cause trouble. Those genuinely seeking information will have let the minister know of the question in advance; often it will be the end of a long line of correspondence with the minister. Sometimes this won't reach the floor of the House and the answer given will be written, not oral. Those wanting to make a point will ask a completely spurious question: 'Would the minister not agree with me that the efforts of Holdsworth Football Club in winning the North East Brewers Cup are a tribute not only to the skills of my constituents but to the confidence they feel playing under New Labour?' The minister then replies, 'Yes, I warmly congratulate the football team in my honourable friend's constituency and agree this is another sign that the North East is prospering under New Labour.' The MP concerned then phones his local paper, or has a drink with its stringer in one of the seventeen bars in Westminster and the paper carries the story – 'Minister Congratulates Holdsworth Eleven'. Hopefully a little goodwill factor may increase the thoughts of the constituency for its Labour member, which, added to all the other little bits of goodwill he is trying to garner, may help him protect his 800 majority at the next general election.

The trouble-making questions are trying to trip the minister up: 'Was the minister responsible for the decision to build a new supermarket at Fairy Cross in my constituency? Has he seen the chaos that has resulted from this? Did he bother to read his Inspector's report on this? Did he bother to take advice? Does he understand the situation? Either he knew what was going on, in which case he is incompetent, or he didn't, in which case he is lazy. Which is it?'

The problem with trouble-making questions, especially those addressed to the Prime Minister by backbenchers, is that they only get one bite of the cherry. This is a classic example of how Parliament works with an unwritten constitution. When PM's questions were twice a week the Leader of the Opposition, by agreement with the Government and the Speaker, through the usual channels, had three goes at asking questions. The Leader of the second largest minority party, the Liberal Democrats, only had one question but asked it, by tradition, when the Leader of the Opposition had finished his questions. When the Labour Government changed this system in 1997, to one session of half an hour instead of two sessions of fifteen minutes, the Leader of the Opposition was allowed six goes, but, if he wanted, could split them to three and later on another three. It was also agreed through the usual channels – organized by the secretary to the Government Chief Whip, a very powerful civil servant working out of 12 Downing Street – that as the Liberal Democrats were now such a large minority party their Leader could have two questions. This was a major advantage. As people see from television the opposition leaders do not really ask questions: they make political points, dressed up as questions by including words such as, 'Will the Prime Minister not agree that ...' Being able to come back a second time means that it is more difficult for a Prime Minister to fob off the questioner. Thus, replying to an opposition backbencher who has spent hours working out an effective soundbite in order to reduce the Prime Minister to a nervous wreck, the PM always wins. Knowing the questioner can't come back on the substantive question he can merely say, 'That is just the kind of stupid question I would expect from the honourable member, and shows very clearly why his party lost the last general election.' He then, skimming through his folder which lists every constituency and next to each a note about what help it has received recently from the Government, adds: 'I would have thought the honourable member would be more concerned about the million pounds subsidy the Government has given his constituency to help rebuild the sewage works. Possibly even a word of thanks to a New Labour government which has done for his constituents what his own party, when in government, should have done years ago.'

No wonder MPs don't take question time seriously. Other than PM's questions when their constituents might turn the television on and wonder if they are not there, attendance is sparse.

Incidentally, note the language. A member of one's own side is an 'honourable friend', of the other side 'honourable member'. They are always 'honourable' in public, no matter what the whips' black book relates. Privy Counsellors, i.e. Cabinet ministers and former Cabinet ministers, are addressed as Right Honourable and by tradition are called to speak before backbenchers. Any lawyer has the tag 'Learned' put in front, and strictly speaking, any former member of the armed services is called 'Gallant'. Harold Wilson said that when he was thinking quickly on his feet it was very useful to drag out the phrase, 'As the Learned and Gallant Right Honourable Member says ...,' and by then he had worked out what to say. Peter Bottomley, when a backbencher, found himself in some confusion when asking questions to his wife Virginia, a minister. ' "Friend" didn't somehow grasp the essential quality of our relationship.' He settled on 'My Right Honourable Kinswoman'.

If backbenchers are frustrated by question time, debates in the chamber can be even worse. Debating time is under the control of the Government, though opposition parties do get 'supply' days to pick their own topics. As far as the Government is concerned, the debating time is there to get their legislation through.

A bill starts off, normally in the House of Commons, but sometimes in the Lords, with a formal first reading of the titles. The second reading will be a debate in the chamber, after question time and business announcements. This could last a few days but can be got through in a matter of hours. The bill then goes to committee stage where it is discussed clause by clause by about fifteen MPs with, of course, the Government having a majority. This reports back to the Commons for a report-stage reading where loose ends are tied up, and there is then a final third reading – when no new material can be introduced. The bill then goes to the Lords where similar stages are gone through, and then goes to the Queen for the Royal Assent and becomes an Act of Parliament.

What chance has a backbencher to make an input? In the main second-reading debate, after time has been taken up by the two front-bench spokespeople opening and summing up, contributions accepted from the smaller parties, privy counsellors called, and those with special constituency interests or personal backgrounds quite rightly catching the Speaker's eye, there is probably time for between ten and fifteen MPs to be called. Balance is kept between the parties but this has to be adjusted to take into account of the size of the government majority – with a very large majority the chances of a government backbencher being called are obviously reduced – and speakers taking a line opposing their own party. The Speaker also takes into account the number of previous contributions an MP has made, the mood of the House, and the time a member spends in the chamber. An MP who makes a speech and then leaves the chamber is unlikely to be called for a very long time. In the same way if an MP has indicated to the Speaker that they would like to be called it is incumbent on courtesy to sit through the whole debate, which might mean seven hours of absolute boredom before he or she gets to their feet with about six people in the House. Only Hansard will report their speech. The serious papers have long since given up offering a summary of the proceedings in Parliament. Not so long ago the broadsheets would have two full pages on business at Westminster. Now, in the age of dumbing down, we get, admittedly often perceptive as well as amusing, sketches. Their party duty whip will make a note in the whips' book and that might help promotion. It will have no effect on government thinking. To have that effect the MP has to get on to the committee. But there the Government has a majority and increasingly with all governments, by the time policy has reached that stage, they are reluctant to change.

The executive has grown both in size and self-importance. There are many more government departments than before and now all ministers who run Cabinet departments, except for Agriculture, Fisheries and Food (for extremely complicated reasons to do with the Dutch and the Privy Council) style themselves Secretaries of State.

A degree of accountability is given by the Select Committees who monitor the activities of departments, but this is generally retro-spective, after policy has been decided upon. Clive Soley, the Labour MP who in the 1990s had charge of the Commons Committee on modernization, is working on plans for ordinary MPs to become more formally involved before legislation is presented to the House and for the House to have easier ways to modify what is seen as bad legislation in practice. But there will be a long struggle to persuade the executive of that. It is not a case of power corrupting, but of power once obtained not lightly given up.

The time to try to change policy is before it is solidified in the Government's mind. That is the lesson presented to those who wish to be effective in policy issues in this country. It is a lesson the established church is learning. As it does so it must ponder the fact that there are advantages and disadvantages in being an established church. It must consider whether, with the Commons being so relatively ineffective with the executive, the channels the established church has inside the system can be used to greater purpose. There is a moral and philosophical question involved in being an established church. There is also an effective question. If Christians wish to be involved in doing God's will in those areas for which we pray for help, are we more likely to be effective in the public domain by being inside or outside the establishment?

6

Parliament: The Lords

IF the House of Commons is the effective part of the Palace of Westminster – and that is a big if – then the House of Lords is certainly the dignified part. Even the way in which the peers vote, 'Content' or 'Not Content', has a disdaining regard for their colleagues in 'another place', the term by which each chamber refers to the other.

Whether that dignity will remain after the reforms carried out by New Labour following their victory in 1997 remains to be seen. One of the reasons for doubt is the lack of clarity of the reforming measures, summed up by the Ninth Marquis of Alsa: 'I don't understand if the Labour Party is reforming us to make the Lords more effective – or less effective.' As with the other constitutional changes – of devolution for Scotland and Wales, elected mayors, regional assemblies, and the UK's changing relationship with the rest of Europe – it seems likely that we are at a starting-point for change, unsure of how developments will proceed. With the hereditary principle altering in the Lords, having an hereditary Supreme Governor and Defender of the Faith as head of the Church of England, and the bishops having 26 seats in the second chamber as of right, with other denominations and faiths having none as a right but only by patronage – with all this, the question of 'establishment' will be on the political (if not the clergy) agenda.

This is not the only reason Christians and those of other faiths should be concerned about the future of the House of Lords. When considering how Christians can be effective, as a church, a group, or individuals, the House of Lords can often be a more rewarding place to start from than the Commons. An understanding of how it works is essential.

There has been much crossfire during the attempts to change the

53

Lords, not only between and within political groupings (the largest group now is the crossbenchers), but also between hereditary and life peers. Lord Cranbourne, from the Salisbury family (who have been involved in front-line politics for over 500 years), put it to Baroness Jay (Labour Leader, life peer and daughter of another life peer, former Prime Minister, James Callaghan): 'None of us in this house is elected. We are all here because of patronage. The difference is my patron is dead and yours is alive. If the country wants an independent second chamber who is more likely to be independent?'

That has always been the nub of the case. While in theory, and always in opposition, political parties argue the case for an independent second chamber, in practice, when in government, parties want a docile second chamber to help get their legislation through. This was recognized by a compromise in the 1911 Parliament Act concerning the powers of the Lords. None of the reforms suggested by New Labour or any of their opponents suggested any serious changes to these powers. The Government steered clear of a directly elected second chamber on the grounds that if both Houses could claim electoral authority there could be gridlock. But the arguments for having some kind of ring-fenced electoral representative system with members from the CBI, the TUC, the Vice-Chancellors, the charities, the regions, etc., are now firmly in the public domain and will not go away. Under this umbrella there will be calls for the position of the churches (all denominations) and other faiths to be reconsidered. The bishops will have to respond.

However reconstruction goes on, the role and function of the Lords is unlikely to be challenged. The 1911 Act restricted the powers of the second chamber to debate and allowed them to refuse bills coming from the Commons up to three times. This gave a chance for a longer and often wider consultation. The advent of life peers in the 1960s meant that both people of distinction from specialist fields and 'working' younger peers who understood the system were now in the House. Often the working peers were needed to put right badly drafted clauses. Life peers could nearly always produce one expert from their own ranks on the subject of debate. When done with courtesy it is a good operational way of the Government rethinking and altering legislation, and responding to new ideas. If there is dispute then after they have rejected a bill three times the Parliament Act is invoked and the bill becomes law – but it rarely comes to that. Since the 1940s the 'Salisbury' (yes, they are a great political family) Convention has been observed. This means that if a measure coming from the Commons has been in the governing party's manifesto then, although the Lords may debate it, they won't vote against it. The Lords cannot refuse finance bills even once.

These measures meant that the, then, biggest problem of the Lords, the original built-in Conservative majority, was, on the whole, contained. Certainly the Conservative peers often proved a thorn in the side of Margaret Thatcher during her premiership. Knowing that whatever one says politically or however little one votes, a seat in the Lords is for life, does produce a great independence of mind. No party whips can see you are deselected in your constituency if you speak against the party line or don't turn up. Of course, if you don't come you can't claim expenses (peers aren't paid).

The Lords has other important functions. Often government bills, normally of a noncontroversial nature, start off in the Lords. This serves as a useful example of how the practice of government has changed. There is now so much legislation. All governments feel that they must introduce bills on almost every aspect of our lives. There just isn't time to start them all off, let alone consider them properly in the Commons. If it is not national legislation being considered there is a constant stream of measures coming from the European Union to be implemented at committee stage. One basic reason for a second chamber is that there is too much business to be voted on, let alone debated properly, by one chamber.

The House of Lords is also the final court of appeal in the land. This is a function which dates back to the twelfth century, when the Commons decided to concern itself with taxation but not legal matters. Originally all peers were involved, but when that became unworkable the Lord Chancellor appointed specific Law Lords. New Labour decided to leave them in place, in spite of some demands that Law Lords and judges should be elected. The growth in stature of the European courts has meant that while the Law Lords are certainly the highest court 'in' the land, they are not necessarily the highest court 'of' the land.

Everyone accepts that there can be no basis in a modern democracy for people having power or influence over the lives of others because of the accident of birth. (Sit down that awkward girl at the back of the class who asks, 'What about the Monarch inheriting the power of being Supreme Governor of the Church of England and having the influence of talking to archbishops?') But with the rapid changing of an institution which has been part of the machinery of government for nearly a thousand years it is worth making a few points which may be overlooked as the new (people's) second chamber develops.

The old House of Lords brought into public life those who were not necessarily interested in politics. Many came from a wider hinterland than the careers based on ambition for office which had been established in the House of Commons. As well as having a wider cross-section of job backgrounds than most of the public realized – as *The Times* reported, 'Only in the British House of Lords could you find a peer who was a bus driver talking on the Transport Bill' – the inherited element meant that both the young and stupid were represented. This was a useful way of bringing the vast majority of highly distinguished life peers down to a practical level. It was also great fun. Because they didn't depend on either public votes or the approval of the whips there was absent the desperate level of competition found in the Commons. They didn't shout and scream across the dispatch box at each other so there was time and space for understanding, tolerance and wit to be displayed. It was a good-humoured House with one peer mentioning, during the debate on *Lady Chatterley's Lover*, that he wouldn't mind his wife reading the book, but he wouldn't want his gamekeeper to get hold of a copy.

In 'another place' the concentration of stories circulating in the bars and tearooms would be about who was moving up; who was going down; who was stabbing whom in the back; who was in trouble with their constituency party. In the Lords, the stories, with personal ambition lacking, were more gentle – often to do with perceived importance and pomposity. I once witnessed an amazing scene when walking down the committee corridor with a Marquis who had taken his seat the day before. He had held a variety of jobs before coming into the title and was happily at home in one of the friendliest bars, the Sports and Social Club, deep in the bowels of Westminster. As in all villages, people would gravitate to the drinking holes that best suited their nature. This one was a real cross-section: MPs, peers, messengers, police, researchers, bishops, etc., but it was frowned on by some not very bright Tories. As we walked along, a Tory backbench peer came galloping up to us, tapped the Marquis on the arm and the following conversation took place:

'Excuse me. You're new, aren't you?'
'Yes. I took my seat yesterday.'
'Well, look. It's a bit like school. Things you have to learn. I must tell you I have heard you have been drinking in the Sports Club. On our side of the House that is something we don't do.'
The Marquis, though a small man, drew himself up to his full height.
'What rank are you?'
'What do you mean?'
'Well, are you a Duke, an Earl, a Viscount, a Baron, or what?'

'Actually, I'm a Baron.'

'Well I'm a fucking Marquis, so piss off.'

Collapse of stout party.

The old Lords added to the gaiety of the nation; no more so than the stories which abounded about the Archbishops. There was one who always insisted on his right to speak first in any debate as his title was at least three hundred years older than any other title in the House. Another supported the hereditary principle because it was awfully useful when dealing with India and Africa as they understood the veneration of elders. The best stories get repeated and changed slightly so that even Nigel Rees of the BBC's *Quote ... Unquote* has trouble verifying the real source. I have heard this after-dinner one used in connection with the last three Archbishops. The Archbishop (whichever one) is talking to the Duke of Edinburgh at a reception in St James'. The Duke asks, 'I don't know, all this promiscuity nowadays. Tell me, Archbishop, do you believe in sex before marriage?'

'No, Sir. Certainly not.'

'Good,' says Edinburgh, 'I'm very glad to hear it. But can you tell me why?'

'Well, Sir. Sex before marriage? Oh no. It tends to delay the start of the service.'

As the nation moves from a more gentle second chamber to what may be a more effective one, a timely salute is paid towards it by John Wells, in his last book before his early death, *The House of Lords – From Saxon Wargods to a Modern Senate: An Anecdotal History*. All the best anecdotes are there, including this one:

> Stuart Braham (one of the Clerks of the House) recalls an amusing encounter when, scorning the sign on the door, he was using the peers' urinal. Believing himself to be alone he released a loud fart, which was greeted to his consternation from inside one of the cubicles by the cry of, 'Dirty bugger!' Humiliated he tiptoed out, passing in the doorway the then Archbishop of Canterbury, Lord Runcie, who innocently took his place at the stalls, leaving the Clerk to imagine the expression on the face of the emerging peer.

A main consideration of a Christian, indeed of all those interested in the place of organized religion in our society, looking at the new House of Lords is the position of the bishops. Why are they there? What do they do? In any sense, does it help Christ?

Historically bishops came into the House of Lords when the third House of Parliament, Convocation – the House of Clergy – was disbanded. They could sit in the Lords without the power of the

Church to tax being compromised as the Lords has never had tax-raising powers. Over the years this became refined and confirmed in the 1911 Act to the two Archbishops; the Bishops of London, Durham and Winchester; and the next 21 most senior bishops. At the start of the 1997 parliamentary session that was: Liverpool, Ripon, Southwark, Lichfield, Exeter, Bristol, Coventry, Norwich, Lincoln, Oxford, Birmingham, Southwell, Blackburn, Carlisle, Ely, Hereford, Leicester, Bath and Wells, Wakefield and Bradford. That left bishops in 23 dioceses waiting in the wings. One hadn't got long to wait: the Bishop of Rochester entered the Lords following David Sheppard's retirement as Bishop of Liverpool. Not that Sheppard left the Lords: he accepted a life peerage and, not surprisingly, took the Labour whip.

As the Prime Minister appoints the archbishops and bishops it can be argued that this is another form of patronage for the second chamber. In theory it is the Monarch who appoints bishops, and D. A. Hunter Johnson, in his book *Church, Synod, State and Crown*, suggests that in practice the Monarch should continue to do so as Head of the Church of England on the advice of bishops, thus by-passing the Prime Minister. The Prime Minister accepts two names from the Church and presents one to the Monarch. During the Thatcher years it was said in the church that if they wanted to make sure their choice got through they put Jim Thompson's (now Bishop of Bath and Wells) name on the list as one of the two.

There has been little call from the clergy to change this system. Yet it could be different. Elevation by accident of seniority might well mean that some regions are not represented. Durham, with around 280 clergy, always has a voice; Manchester, with over 330, is on the 'hit-or-miss' list. There has been no great consideration of offering to the House of Lords a system whereby the Church of England decides for itself which bishops sit, perhaps on a rota basis. Indeed might not a better system be if not all the sitting clergy were bishops? Why hasn't change been proposed? First, because those enjoying a perceived advantage are normally reluctant to give that up. Second, because the most common comment is, 'Does it really matter?' Yes it does. If only on the grounds that if it really doesn't matter, for God's sake abolish it. The Church of England has enough to do without cluttering itself up with things that don't matter just so that a few bishops can sit in the Lords. They do have one perceived disadvantage, which Anthony Trollope appreciated: they are the only members of the House of Lords whose wives cannot style themselves 'Lady'.

However, there can be definite advantages for the bishops, the

Church of England and the nation, in their attendance at the House of Lords. The first one is simple. There is a duty bishop who leads prayers for good government at the start of each day's business in the Lords. Either prayers mean something or they don't. If, as Christians, we believe that they do then this must be useful, even if only by concentrating their Lordships' minds on where their duty lies.

It also gives bishops somewhere to go. Most bishops get involved in hectic schedules of meetings, committees, visits, trouble-shooting. Even if they have tremendous support from families and staff it is still a lonely position. Clergy in their diocese have other clergy to talk with. The bishop must be careful not to be seen to have special friends, and it is difficult to have other equal working friends. This has been especially true since the Second World War. Before that the background of a bishop would, generally speaking, be similar to that of the Lord Lieutenant, the High Sheriff, the Member of Parliament, the Commanding Officer of the County Regiment. He would fit happily into an upper-middle-class social mix. That would be his support group. But it is no longer true, though an understanding of that change has not reached a wider public.

Going to the Lords means that a bishop has a legitimate reason for being away from the problems of the diocese; a chance to reflect relaxing on the red benches of the chamber and an opportunity to talk, away from prying ears and eyes, with other bishops – and other parliamentarians and journalists, on lobby terms.

However, the greatest advantage should be what the bishops can give. They offer Christian witness at the Palace of Westminster and they are able to offer individual Christian views both formally in debate and off the record in private conversations. This should make an impact. The question is how effective are they and should they be trying to make a greater impression?

There is one further way in which the Church of England is intertwined with Parliament at Westminster and that is through the Ecclesiastical Committee. This is a unique standing committee of Parliament because it is comprised of members of both Houses. Its function is to consider all matters concerning the governing and operation of the Church of England, and especially to look at measures coming from the General Synod which need parliamentary approval. Meetings are held between the Committee and representatives of Synod. The Ecclesiastical Committee has the responsibility of reaching a view which it feels reflects the opinion of Parliament as a whole (note Parliament: not Government). This often means some kind of compromise and at times the politicians have felt that the

Synod has not fully taken into account the different audience they are dealing with at Westminster, compared with an audience of committed Christians.

All Christians should understand that if they wish to have an influence on changing the most significant factors in the Church of England then this is a key committee with which to deal. It has a statutory role and the names of its members are published. Because it represents both Houses it can be approached either through Members of Parliament or peers. As with so many areas of campaigning it is often more productive to approach Parliament via the Lords rather than the Commons. That was certainly true for the old House of Lords. Whatever else changes, nothing suggests that will.

7

The Government of the Church of England

MOST observers will tell you that the average person in the pew has little real idea about the government of the Church of England. Not that the clergy complain. In fact some will go so far as to say that if the punter isn't making a fuss and is blissfully unaware as to what is going on then all must be well and they must be doing something right. In many ways the government of the Church is the exact opposite of the government of the nation. In politics, even paid-up members of a party will have little contact with their MP. But they will see and hear the Leader of their party nightly on television. In the church, members of the congregation will see their incumbent every week but rarely see their bishop on television, and the Archbishops only on special media occasions. Perhaps it is that close link at parish level which negates a desire for more knowledge about how the Church of England is run. Perhaps it is also the history of obedience that has run through the Christian churches that has led to many people not wishing to become involved in decision-making. I say 'many' because it is not the case for those who, for a variety of reasons, offer their time and talents to committees, working parties and focus groups.

Decision-making in religious matters is a tricky affair, summed up for me by a student at a conference who asked, 'Is God a democrat?' If the apostolic succession is meaningful are not some things decreed by God and handed down through the bishops, not to be questioned by congregations? If so – which things? The virgin birth? Transfiguration? The ordination of women? The sanctity of marriage? Homosexual priests? Sharing mass with other denominations? Having a Supreme Governor and Defender of Our Faith who is also Defender of All Faiths? (Incidentally if Prince Charles does take on that mantle the question must be asked from where does his authority stem?) There is ample ground for confusion here as to who has responsibility for what.

Most members of the Church of England will know that they have church wardens and parish councils (called Parochial Church Councils and not to be confused with the local government ones) and that they send members, sometimes via a deanery synod, to a synod of the diocese and then perhaps on to the General Synod. This produces reports and holds debates and can affect their form of worship (often it seems as though this has been done with too little consultation as far as they personally are concerned). They know that there are a whole range of committees at every level but most are not entirely sure of the powers of the wardens or PCC, especially when it comes to appointing a new vicar. Nor are most sure of the powers of their bishop, or patron, in this matter.

When it comes to policy issues, members of local churches know from the newspapers and television and from visiting preachers that 'the church' rarely has one agreed policy on any matter and that, on the whole, most clergy can say what they want. Over the years, from John Robinson, when Bishop of Woolwich, to David Jenkins, when Bishop of Durham, they have got used to those taking an unorthodox line, enjoying a high media profile and getting into all kinds of spats with other clerics and MPs but without being sat on by the Archbishops.

The public has also seen the disputes and confusions about who is actually responsible for – and more importantly settles arguments in – cathedrals and Royal Peculiars. The rows in recent years at Lincoln and Westminster would do credit to Trollope. One rector put it to me like this: 'All the time you are in charge of something and looking after it no one wants to know. As soon as you say you are going to sell it all kinds of people and committees come out of the woodwork and say that actually it's their responsibility.'

So, the confusion about who should hold moral responsibility in the church is compounded by who actually owns and takes responsibility for artifacts and fabrics. The Church of England has so many, not necessarily out-of-date, laws whose legitimacy can now well be questioned. What it hasn't got is the people, the time, the resources, or the operational procedure to do this speedily and effectively. This understandably can cause disquiet if not outrage from laity and clergy alike. Here are two specific examples picked from a host of many which will be found by anyone taking a close look at the parishes of the Church of England. I have selected one from the clergy and one from the laity. The clergy first; a letter to the *Daily Telegraph*, on

Friday 30 April 1999. It was printed under the heading, 'Apostles needn't apply':

> Sir – On attempting to elect as church warden an American citizen who was in every respect the obvious candidate, the parish of Hartley Wintney has fallen foul of an 18th century law of England. This forbids Jews and aliens and those who have committed some felony for standing for office.
>
> Clearly the law is an ass, and the sooner it is repealed the better. We are in good comfort that should, our lord himself, St. Paul or any of the apostles have presented themselves as candidates they would also have been excluded.
>
> Canon Robin Ewbank, Hook, Hants.

The other example is also from a published source and therefore already in the public domain. It is from the village magazine of the Chiddingstones in Kent, dated March 1999. This article appears under the heading, 'From the Church Wardens' Confessional':

> Outwardly things may not have appeared to have changed very much during the last month but under the surface the Church of England, in the form of our Diocese, has begun to stir.
>
> The question most often posed to us is, 'Have we got a new Rector yet?' The answer we have to give is 'no' and unless you are intimately connected with the workings of the Church it must seem odd that our previous Rector has been gone several months and there is no sign of a replacement. Indeed it has been quite amazing to those of us who thought we did know the ins and outs of it.
>
> A Rector or Vicar has a freehold on his, or her, parish and can not be moved until they decide to move on, or reach retirement age, or do something incredibly naughty. To avoid finding itself in a situation where unsuitable clergy are in place for life the Church usually appoints a Priest-in-Charge. When our previous Rector arrived he held this post (Priest-in-Charge) for five years at which time the situation has to be reviewed by law. He then became Rector for the next nine years until his departure. So he has gone, and no-one has been appointed to replace him, why not? This was the question we asked ourselves many times. We believed that we would be able to draw up a Parish Profile, that's like a CV in reverse, where the parish tells what it wants from possible applicants; advertise the vacancy and put a successful applicant forward to the Bishop for his approval; just as happened when our previous Rector was head-hunted and presented to the then Bishop. The Church, like most of modern life, has its problems, not the least of which is a shortage of clergy. Rochester has more than its fair share of clergy and other dioceses have been making it quite clear that they want more of the action, so we will have to shed some of our manpower and

womanpower. Add to this the fact that a good many clergy are leaving this Deanery, or locality, and mother Church sees an opportunity to take an 'overview', their word not ours, and not the only business sounding word being used by our diocese. It is not quite Rochester plc but it sometimes sounds like it, and this in turn is caused by the shrinkage in the number of clergy and the necessity of those remaining to become better managers of their resources.

On Monday 15th February 1999, and with all these facts in the background, the Combined Parochial Church Councils, or PCCs, met with the Bishop of Tonbridge, who was the representative of the Bishop of Rochester, the Archdeacon of Tonbridge, the Rural Dean and the Lay Chairman of the Deanery.

The purpose of the meeting was to allow members of the PCCs to question the visitors and, very importantly, to decide whether it was the wish of the members that, 'the presentation of the benefice be suspended'. At this point our Patron, the Archbishop of Canterbury, becomes involved as it is he who in theory presents a candidate to the Bishop of Rochester to be our Rector. As we do not want a Rector straight away without having to see what she or he is like for the first five years or so, it is necessary for the Archbishop to waive his right to present a candidate. Reluctantly it was the unanimous decision of those present that we agree to this move.

Reading between the lines, 'The Rector gone for several months and no sign of a replacement', and 'the question we asked ourselves many times', the clear sense of frustration and of being left in the dark comes through; made more pointedly by being expressed in the measured tones of responsible church wardens.

The feeling of not quite knowing what is going on, that something is being stitched up behind the scenes, is not confined to local people concerned with local issues. At national level the Church of England and some of its respective parts can often give the impression that it prefers to do things out of the public gaze. There are many reasons for this. One is the hierarchical system through which the church developed and which is still seen clearly in many religious and quasi-religious establishments: church schools, monasteries, convents, the Salvation Army, etc. It is not long ago that priests were telling women not to come to church services in trousers. They preside over their own services. They serve 'under' their bishop who in turn comes under either Canterbury or York. There has not been a tradition of a questioning culture. Indeed, exactly the opposite. The laity and junior clergy has gone to the senior clergy for advice and guidance. It makes it difficult, given that background, to develop an inquiring mind into the activities of the church.

This has produced, not just in some clergy but also in some high-ranking lay figures, an attitude that they do not need to explain their actions let alone consult with their juniors before taking them. It is almost as though a subconscious mindset develops of: God, arch-bishop, bishop, clergy, laity, with each having a 'will' and not needing to explain it to those perceived to be below.

This is not to suggest this state is deliberate, or anyone's fault. It is just that in this kind of atmosphere it is hard to conceive a sensitive, courteous and questioning approach. So often the questioning, when it does come, is too late and in the form of bloody-minded individuals not really searching for truth and trying to be helpful but just out to make trouble.

It must be stressed this is not just the clergy. The biggest shock to the system of 'they are in charge; leave them alone; they know what they are doing' came in 1992 when the Church of England collectively realized that the Church Commissioners had been left unquestioned for years looking after our £3 billion of property, land and Stock Exchange portfolio, and had lost £80 million.

When that happened there were three immediate reactions throughout the church. One was, how was this allowed to happen? The second was, to whom are the Church Commissioners accountable and how do they bolt on to the structure of the diocese, the bishops, General Synod and Parliament? The third was, if the church was so rich why do we keep on having to have fundraising mornings for the repair of the steeple?

The view from the pew on the government of the church is hazy. People only begin to peer through that haze when something goes wrong. The basic principles of government of the church are rarely discussed at parish level, either in the pulpit or at meetings of the PCC. The assumption is that in theory the essential unit is the parish and the relationship between priest and congregation. Continuing that same theory all other activities and organizations should be used to strengthen that base. But in practice the growth of structures, management overviews, the need for top-level relationships with Government and national and international organizations has meant that in some cases the growth of bureaucracy and the natural human vested interest in empire-building has resulted in the tail wagging the dog. In a great many cases the view of the diocese from the parish is not one of grateful thanks for what they are getting but one of irritation and annoyance at the forms they have to fill in, the meetings they have to attend, and the money they have to raise for activities and people not directly involved in parish work. The Chiddingstones article above showed that they didn't see any direct help coming to them from the diocese – only a plea to take on trust the belief that the diocese 'overview' was correct.

This is an organizational problem which affects many areas of life. It may well be in many cases, as far as the church is concerned, unfair, with the fault not in substance but in failure of communication. I suggested that to one vicar and she immediately exclaimed, 'Don't tell them that. They will just argue the case for appointing another information officer – and we will have to raise money for that.'

Do people really know where power, decision-making, responsibility and accountability lie in the Church of England? Are the relationships between archbishops, bishops, clergy, laity, plus Government, General Synod, the Commissioners, and the secretariats at Church House and Lambeth Palace, clear? The government of the Church of England should only exist to enable the church to carry out its agreed functions. But what are the functions of the church and are they agreed?

The definitions of the function of the church are many and varied. One could happily spend a term in the Bodleian Library researching the definitions and still have much work to do; there are over 2 million references on the internet alone. Accepting that, let's start with a definition from Robert Runcie, Archbishop of Canterbury, in 1980:

> If you were to ask me where I think the emphasis should be as we consider the question of what the church is for and how it ought to conduct its mission, I would say the first priority is to strengthen ordinary church members in a gospel way of looking at the world and of living their own lives. The accent should be on positive and affirmative Christian teaching in our congregations.

It seems to me we can draw three distinct but overlapping functions from these words:

1 The church exists to strengthen Christians. It is a corporate body to strengthen, partly by togetherness, Christians' worship, work and witness.
2 The church has a duty to conduct mission. The world gives many examples of how this may be done, from hard-sell international projects to the welcoming warmth and openness of a local congregation.
3 To enable Christians to look at the world and to live their own lives in a gospel way. That means helping us to live to the standards in

which we believe, even when we have to cope with failure. We must also recognize that we are part of the whole world, in which we should adopt a 'gospel way of looking'. That is, we become the tools of Christ in all aspects of the life of the world.

Taking that as a broad definition of the functions of the church, the next step is to consider how the Church of England develops its structures, organization and decision-making – its government – to meet those ends.

The key body is the congregation, meeting and evolving around the Gospels. That means a place to meet and access to a priest. Already, just by that simple statement, other factors in the Archbishop's definition come into play: the priest must be licensed by a bishop; the church must have resources for a continuing examination of the Gospels and their application in a changing world. Because this definition is not a blueprint but is dealing with an organization that has grown up over 2000 years, there are matters of history and involvement with the secular world that have to be taken into account. It means management and organization structures, in practice away from the parish, but in theory, and in hope, to help the parish.

Parishes need priests. Priests must be educated and trained and supported. A structure outside the parish is needed for that. Priests have to preach the gospel. But the Gospels themselves pose the following problems:

- Did the historical incident described actually happen?
- Is the translation of that incident correct?
- Is the interpretation from that translation right?
- Is that interpretation correctly understood?

Raising these questions suggests that degrees of intelligence and research are needed to be a Christian. This runs completely counter to the whole concept of faith on which the religion is founded and is therefore obviously nonsense. Yet, our faith is based on the Gospels, which we are encouraged to read and ponder. So there must be scholars working at the sharp end of history, language and teaching, and the church must provide a structure for that.

From an example of theory to an example of practice with which the church has to deal – cathedrals, with Royal Peculiars, such as Westminster Abbey, shortly coming under the Church of England's umbrella. There are difficult decisions here. Built to the glory of God as places of worship, many now act as the management and education centre of their diocese, as well as being major tourist attractions and in need of constant funds for upkeep. How the cathedral authorities deal with visitors is of the highest importance. For many tourists this is one of their few direct contacts with Christian centres and Christian people. Flood the building with too many tourists and often the essential elements are lost. Charge them too much money – indeed give the impression that their visit is all about making money from them – and the more articulate will stump off muttering about Jesus throwing the money-changers out of the Temple. Have the cathedral staffed by untrained, bossy and insensitive people and the whole exercise of allowing tourists in can be counter-productive in a big way. Give them a good Christian experience and they may go home and visit their parish church. All this needs a management structure.

These two examples, of Gospel scholarship and crowd control impacting with the outside world, show that the government of the church must spread outside the parish structure. For Christians who wish to be effective in 'looking at the world' and be active in making an impression there is a need to understand the government of their own church before coming to a decision as to whether it is better to work for change inside, or outside.

At the start of the twenty-first century the Church of England will consist of around 16,000 churches open for worship, over 10,000 clergy (over 1000 of them women), and 105 bishops. It will attract a regular worshipping population of around 4 per cent, while at least half the population will at some point in their lives claim to be nominal Christians. The whole public nature of the church at any one time is expressed by the personality, sayings, writings and activities of the Archbishop of Canterbury. The Archbishop is one of the few people in the country whose job is safe for as long as he wishes to hold it. Unlike Prime Ministers, leaders of industry, trades union bosses, even judges and other clergy, there is no one with any knowledge of the constitutional machinery which would be needed to sack an archbishop. The Archbishop is served by a secretariat at Lambeth Palace as well as in his own see at Canterbury. Lambeth Palace has considerable authority – it is the only non-university in the world to be able to confer its own degrees. Indeed it has such authority that the building now ranks with Buckingham Palace and Number 10 Downing Street as one of those few structures in the country able to make public pronouncements, so that the papers are quite likely to carry a quote, 'Lambeth Palace said ...', when the church wants to issue a statement not as the personal thoughts of the Archbishop but as the view of the church authorized by the Archbishop but not stepping on any ground which should be reserved for opinions from Church House. Church House, which is the secretariat for the workings of the General Synod, is also empowered to make statements on behalf of the Church of England, but reflecting the collective view of the Synod and not that of the Archbishop.

The Synod is the parliament of the church. It takes to the Palace of Westminster those things the church wants altered or approved by Act of Parliament: the prayer books, the powers of church wardens, the tax status of the church, the classification (or not) of clergy as self-employed, etc. It also sets up boards to consider specific issues where it feels the church has expertise or responsibility. Most of this work is directed through the Board for Social Responsibility (BSR) and the Board of Education where the church, in its own words, tries 'to speak for an undifferentiated public good over and against more partial interests'.

Both the Synod and the Archbishop directly from time to time commission reports. These either stem from feelings inside the church or from pressure on the Archbishop or Synod from lobbies. There is no overall plan with a permanent monitoring system on the life of the nation. Most of these reports – like most government reports – disappear without trace. Occasionally they coincide with the mood of the nation, such as *Faith in the City*, which was commissioned directly by the Archbishop, Robert Runcie, in 1983. This looked at Urban Priority Areas and the problems of housing, social care, and education. It had a wide impact on members of the church, Government, political parties, those working in the field, and the general public. Its thinking set the benchmark for thought and activity for years to come.

'Bolted on' to the General Synod are the Church Commissioners. Up until the scandal of the early 1990s the only working relationship was once a year when the 95 Commissioners submitted their Annual Financial Report. Rationalization of the position and role of the Commissioners is now an ongoing scrutiny.

The Commission in its current form grew out of the 1836 Act of Parliament to reorganize the income of the church, basically to move it away from the bishops to where it was needed. The two Archbishops became the Ecclesiastical Commissioners and there were five senior Cabinet ministers, including the Prime Minister, as ex-officio members. The First Church Estates Commissioner, who was the key decision-maker, was appointed by the Monarch on the advice of the Prime Minister and in practice worked not to the other Commissioners but directly to the Archbishop of Canterbury.

Until the calamities happened most people in the pew were not concerned overmuch with the big picture of church finance. The Bishop of Coventry, Simon Barrington-Ward, gave the situation a welcome as it caused 'the people in the parishes to come alive to the Gospel and see the need to give for the cause which really should be at the heart of their lives'. Was he being ironic?

Those campaigning Christians who wish to work through and with the government of the church as individuals or groups have the problem of the democratic ceiling. They can get elected up to General Synod level – and a lot of valuable lobbying work on local issues can be done at parish, or deanery level – and can probably get working parties established. But the only democratic say they have over senior appointments is using influence, not votes, to persuade the church over which names to offer to the Prime Minister. In theory, of course, they have a say by a voting system which decides which party leader becomes Prime Minister and advises the Queen on who to make Archbishop, assuming a vacancy occurs during his or her tenure in Downing Street. But that is tortuous democracy.

8

Public Praying and Campaigning: The Issues

THOSE listening to intercessions week by week in our parish churches will know that some areas of public life are offered to God as expressions of our concern for his creation. War, terror, large-scale human and natural disaster, individual and collective worries about health and education, are always high on the agenda, as is more recently Third World debt.

Some areas of life, unless there is immediate local appeal, tend not to be brought before God. Taxation is rarely mentioned, not even in the context of improving the lot of the National Health Service and the caring professions. Integrated transport policy almost never gets a mention. It seems to be felt that even constitutional changes would be of no interest to God, and didn't require his help. In fact it is possible to go through the list of Cabinet responsibilities and note which ones are likely to make the intercession list on a fairly regular basis:

Prime Minister's Office	No
Deputy Prime Minister's Office	
– Regions	No
– Environment	Yes
– Transport	No
Lord Chancellor's Office	No
Foreign Office (trouble spots)	Yes
Chancellor of Exchequer's Office	No
Home Office (race, immigration and prisons)	Yes
Board of Trade	No
Defence (in war time)	Yes
Constitutional Matters	No
Heritage	No

Education/Employment	Yes
Social Security	Yes
Education	Yes
Scotland	No
Wales	No
Northern Ireland	Yes
Health	Yes
Agriculture	No
International Development	Yes

There will of course be local and regional variations, but there does seem to be a pattern of mainly including in our public prayers those activities for which the church has been historically involved, such as education; or which stem directly from the ministry of Christ, concerns with health, suffering and potential suffering.

This produces an interesting situation whereby sometimes some Christians get involved in campaigning for issues in the world which the church is not offering to God in the spirit of seeking helpful advice. This was a concern of John Gummer, in a book he wrote with Eric Heffer and Alan Beith, *Faith in Politics* (1987). A Conservative MP, a Labour MP and a Liberal Democrat MP – all Christians, presenting their views to the electorate before a general election. Gummer wrote:

> Politicians have been concerned at the decline in rural transport and have sought ways of improving the opportunities for those in the country who have no access to cars. As a Conservative Government sought to bring more operators and greater competition into the routes, so the argument has been crystallised into one about deregulation. The Church has obviously a contribution to the discussion. It is a voice for those who might otherwise have been forgotten and it does have a good deal of understanding about rural life with its network of country parishes and village churches. It would therefore be perfectly proper for a bishop to remind the government of its responsibilities to the poor and to see that the demands of the gospel had an impact upon the decisions which were being made. Yet the Bishop of Durham went much further. He suggested that deregulation was not a policy which Christians could support.

These were not the terms in which the Bishop would have addressed a public prayer to God.

In his chapter Gummer gives the impression that because the church has never shown any detailed expertise on transport policy it is perfectly all right for the Bishop to show general concern, but he should stop short of suggesting any particular course of action. This is a recurrent difficulty for those who lead public prayer, well highlighted by the Labour Party's theme song for the 1997 general election, 'Things can only get better'. Fine. Great words. It is only when one moves on to specify how you intend to make things better that trouble starts.

Pray to improve the health of the nation and all will respond, 'Hear our prayer'. Specifically pray for the government to ban all tobacco products, alcoholic drinks and sugar, and half the congregation will be saying under their breath, 'Hey, wait a minute'.

Where the church speaks publicly to God, and where it wishes to play a part in national life, it is on much stronger ground when it concentrates on those areas where it can offer experience. It was a pity that the voice of the church was so quiet during the debate on devolution in the United Kingdom. For the church has relevant experience. Working with the disestablished churches in Wales and Scotland it could have offered real help not just to the Government but to the British people, had it been asked – or had it had the confidence to put its own experience, expertise and views forward.

The church was not in the past so comparatively timid in public life. In many areas it has a much longer history of involvement than the state. Hospitals, orphanages, schools, colleges were all originally established by charities, endowments or individuals from Christian backgrounds. Only in the last century did the state start to play a major role. In education it was very much to supplement what the church was doing, providing National schools where there were not any church ones, rather than replace church provision.

It is in the institutions of education that Christianity has its most noticeable impact after the actual buildings of the church. Certainly more so than the armed services, prisons, hospitals or industry. Of the 26,000 publicly maintained primary and secondary schools in the UK over 7000 are classified as 'voluntary', of which over 4000 are 'aided', that is, running costs are met by either local or national government, but the buildings are the responsibility of the voluntary bodies. In most cases, in almost all of the voluntary schools the voluntary body is a religious denomination. The majority of the 2300 independent schools have strong religious connections, many having their own chaplains.

The Christian context is far wider than that. Skim the lists of schools in a local telephone book and by far the largest group will have names starting with 'St'. The transforming 1944 Butler Education Act decreed that all schools should start the day with a collective act of Christian worship. Long before the national curriculum was even a twinkle in Margaret Thatcher's eye, statute laid down that the one subject that had to be taught in state schools was religious education. By the time the various and changing authors – politicians, civil servants and academics alike – had realized that the production of a national curriculum was an ongoing tortuous process the place of religious education was proving a problem. There was no solution, merely a piece of official nonsense broad enough to be meaningless, but providing for schools to by-pass the 1944 Act if they wished. A quote from *Whitaker's Almanack* sums it up well: 'Religious education, although not prescribed by the national curriculum, is a requirement across all key stages; the syllabus is devised locally and parents have the right to remove their children if they wish.'

The provisions for the daily assembly were also by-passed, depending on the attitude of the head teacher. Where he or she were committed Christians they did their best. Some non-believers went through the motions with a damaging degree of mockery. Some Christians and non-believers alike seized the opportunity to use this as an inspiring and imaginative corporate occasion, and some schools in multiracial areas used their initiative to direct the assembly into exploration and tolerance.

The churches, the church schools, the education advisors in the dioceses, the Sunday schools (or whatever name is used), teachers and pupils who are church attenders – these all provide a network for the church. This can be used to gather information, to pass on information, to offer advice, as a basis for campaigning and praying. But it needs to be brought together using the churches' historical stimulus of involvement and expertise.

This is as true for shaping our prayers as it is for lobbying. Too often in public intercessions we offer general prayers for teachers and specifically named schools, or we pray for 'All those about to take important exams'. What are we asking God to do here? We are not praying for favouritism for children from our particular church. So we are praying for children to do of their best in exams. I wonder if we have thought that through. It seems to me that there are dangers in this approach. What about those children who are not doing exams – who perhaps are not deemed suitable by their schools to sit important exams? Are we not somehow side-lining them? Once this point is raised then, of course, the response is, 'Oh, we will pray for them as well'. But the fact is that wasn't our first thought. Secondly, in many cases the pressure on young people taking exams, which may decide university entrance, is so great that it does them no good to hear themselves singled out in a church service for special prayers. One seventeen-year-old said to me, 'As I heard the intercessions I thought oh, no. Now if I don't do well, not only will I have let down myself, my parents and my school. I will have let God down as well.' And allowance must also be made for those who don't do well (comparing themselves with their friends who have), in an understandably traumatic state, who wonder what they have done to upset God that he has replied to public prayers in this public way.

So, how should the church go about praying in its area of expertise, in education. I think it should look hard at the state of education, using its networking advantages and pray (and organize and campaign) to be effective in those areas where it feels it can help with solutions.

There is one area highlighted by the problems of establishing a national curriculum that cries out to be examined and prayed for. That is a consideration of the knowledge explosion and how it should be coped with in schools. I have a set of Harmsworth's Universal Encyclopedia: nine volumes, first published in 1915, updated in the 1930s, which starts with the German town of 'Aachen' and goes on to the Finnish tribe 'Zyrians'. All knowledge then known contained therein. Compare that with the present. Two-thirds of all books ever written have been published since 1980. The amount of research, not just in new technical subjects, but also in subjects like history and English literature, is growing constantly. Knowledge is being discovered about parts of the world and the universe which were unimaginable a few years ago. Access to material on the internet is doubling at a faster and faster rate.

It is no longer possible either to produce a nine-volume encyclopedia containing all one needs to know, or for one person or a committee to sit down and say, 'This is what is known. From this we will select what children should be taught.' Those days have gone for good and that is why all attempts to produce a national curriculum will fail, and result in added stress. Children are at school for around forty hours a week. English, maths, science (chemistry, biology, physics, zoology), information technology, foreign languages, classics, history, geography, economics, music, art (painting, sculpture, graphics, textiles), drama, film studies, media studies, religious studies, games, physical education – there is no end to it, let alone time to be involved in clubs and societies and to experience private study.

Added to that is the government demand for citizenship to be taught. That is where the church should pray it can make a contribution.

The second major area that comes up for prayers in public intercession is that of suffering, in all its many forms. Churches have a long and noble tradition, dating back to Christ, of concern for the sick. This is especially true at local level where clergy and often laity work closely with hospitals and hospices. There is a real identification in the prayers with members of congregations who are ill. Most parishes try to have a wider network operating so that those who are suffering but are not immediate members of the congregation have access to the resources of the church if they so wish. Churches will take on board any pressing local issues, such as the changing pattern of care offered by the National Health Service and the local authorities, but on the whole they tend not to have the interest or the resources to keep a running monitor on the development of the NHS. When government changes are proposed or factors affecting the running of the service are highlighted in the media these tend not to be offered to God in prayer. Yet the church has valuable experience here which, with God's help, could be offered to the nation. For example, there is much debate at present about the pragmatic need to ration treatments and medicines to cope with the continuing growing demand on the NHS. In many cases this has taken the form of either openly, but more often covertly, limiting services to the elderly. In a great many parishes the elderly and articulate, with direct experience of the NHS, form a high proportion of the congregations. The church could provide an opportunity for their voice to be heard.

There is an ongoing debate about euthanasia. Christian doctors working with the hospice movement have probably got the greatest and most valid expertise available in the country. This is a topic which could be brought before God in prayer and also placed before both opinion-formers and the general public.

Suffering is not just about illness and, as David Sheppard so tellingly wrote in *Bias to the Poor*, we have a duty of concern to those who suffer from poverty, both at home and abroad. The church needs to pray to avoid charges of confusion, arrogance and naivety here. Fundamental problems are addressed by the Bishop of Oxford, Richard Harries, in *Is There a Gospel for the Rich?* The church has always had moral problems about means and ends. For example, a simple question such as should the church raise money itself to help the poor by collecting rents from property used for prostitution raises all kinds of other questions about responsibility and care.

There are a great many economic activities of which most Christians would not approve, say, making money from tobacco products, selling weapons, pornography, Third World sweat shops. The realization that a blanket ban on the commercial activities of all those listed by Christians as being wrong would actually result in more immediate unemployment and therefore poverty, stresses the need for care in thought – prayer offered to God, and in action – campaigning to the Government. Not to show awareness of the economic complexities may lead to not being taken seriously with views that deserve to be heard. There are a wide variety of opinions on this subject. Some agree with Richard Harries that, 'The market economy both nationally and internationally can indeed be under-pinned by Christian values.' Many agree with Eric Heffer, represen-tative of a strong strand of Christian socialism, that, 'It is the very system which is wrong, and what is required is a fundamental change in the system – not just some tinkering about with controls in the City to stop the worst abuses, but a society where such an institution as the City would be superfluous.'

The church has to accept that it has a pluralistic outlook on this and pray for guidance that this pluralism does not lead to a neutralization of effectiveness.

One area where that has not happened is in the Church of England's involvement with other churches and other organizations in the campaign to deal with Third World debt. Questions may be raised about the strategy and tactics of the lobbying but the church seems to have successfully dealt with bringing forward a single-issue topic from a pluralistic background.

Otherwise foreign affairs tends not to get mentioned in prayers unless one of the world's trouble spots is in the news. On the principle, I suppose, of 'if it ain't broke don't try and fix it'. This means that intercessions on overseas matters are led from media reports and don't have the same impact as prayers relating to activities seen, experienced or known about at first hand. Perhaps there is scope here for the world-wide network of churches to work more closely together at an inter-reporting level. At the moment a lot of what comes from churches internationally is very worthy, but mighty boring.

The classic example of people who only get prayed for when they are in the news is the armed forces. It was ever thus. Kipling wrote:

O it's Tommy this, an' Tommy that, an' 'Tommy, go away';
But it's 'Thank you, Mister Atkins', when the band begins to play,
[...]
For it's Tommy this, an' Tommy that, an' 'Chuck him out, the brute!'
But it's, 'Saviour of 'is country' when the guns begin to shoot;

The varied positions of those in the church are as marked in a consideration of defence as of economic matters. Some Christians are pacifists (but of course not all pacifists are Christians). Some Christians are confused. Those who believe in the concept of a just war are sometimes those who would rather the church didn't invest in armaments – as though it would somehow help you to be victorious in a just war if your services were less well armed and not so able to defend themselves as the enemy.

In fact, it has been the topic of defence (together with urban poverty and race and immigration) on which the church has been loudest in public debate in the second half of the twentieth century. This has been partly because the media liked focusing on the actions of two clergymen: Canon Collins and the Roman Catholic Bruce Kent, leaders of the Campaign for Nuclear Disarmament. To those not around in the 1950s, 1960s and 1970s, it is difficult to give a picture of the passion that the subject of nuclear defence aroused – marches, sit-ins, reports, debates, meetings ending in tears and fighting. On the surface a public discussion about the pros and cons of either multi-national or unilateral nuclear disarmament, but underneath a disturbing residue of political hatred. The General Synod debating a report on *The Church and the Bomb* did what the Church of England is accused many times of doing, of nailing its colours firmly to the fence. In *The Church and Politics Today* (edited by George Moyser), John Elford, Lecturer in Social Ethics at the University of Manchester, writes:

> The outcome of this debate (1982) probably reflects the current state of general opinion in the Church of England about nuclear defence policy. It is opposed to the unilateral renunciation of all nuclear weapons whatever the consequences and is also uneasy about supporting without qualification the present state of affairs.

The debate in the country and the church is worthy of mentioning for two reasons. It showed the Church of England, whatever answers it failed to come to, prepared to engage in a subject of intense public interest, and as such provides a role model to be examined for lessons to be learnt. It also shows how public debate always takes place in an historical context. Then the Cold War and the deterrent effect of the nuclear bomb was of vital interest. At the end of the century the Cold War has collapsed and the public debate has melted away, even though most of the stockpiles of weapons are still there. There is absolutely no interest shown in re-opening a debate about nuclear defence. We have moved on.

Clergy who were active at that time and are still in practice now say that one difference between the nuclear issue and all matters of race is that forming the prayers is easier. There were many sides to the nuclear debate, so clergy had to adopt a safe prayer policy of asking God for his guidance to do his will, without publicly expressing their own opinions. On race, that has never been a difficulty. The church clearly follows Christ's instruction to be on the side of the oppressed. Although coming to the public debate late – the first debate on the subject was not held in General Synod until the 1970s – the church, by prayer, national comment and positive local action, has been one of the most effective players. It has spoken with one voice and has recently developed a strategy following the Stephen Lawrence tragedy of increased concern and involvement.

The Churches Commission for Racial Justice held a conference at Westminster Central Hall on 24 March 1999 on race relations, in the wake of the Stephen Lawrence enquiry. Rev. Robert Day, one of those attending, said:

> The Report has revealed new things about the nature of racism in Britain, particularly that subtle forms of racism are just as damaging as overt forms. The police were not wilfully racist in open ways, but they were unwittingly racist. The finer points of the case reveal negligence of the victim and his family and dismissal of certain pieces of evidence arising from inexcusable ignorance and insensitivity in racial matters.
>
> We can now recognise what should have been obvious all along – that the structures of our institutions and the attitudes and assumptions formed within them perpetuate subtle forms of racism. The police are no more nor less racist than British institutions in general. The Church does well to learn from the mistakes made by the police, since we almost certainly make similar mistakes ourselves.

This was a useful conference, attended by Christians of all cultural, ethnic and denominational shades. Neville Lawrence, the murdered boy's father, said it was a chance to change the fact that, 'This society has turned its back on the Church as a place of information and formation.' Richard Harries, the Bishop of Oxford, confirmed his belief that, 'The Church is ideally placed to tackle the issue of racism, because of its belief in redemptive love and the oneness of human beings.' John Sentamu, the Bishop of Stepney, expressed his willingness to work with (and not against) the police: 'My attitude towards the police is one of critical solidarity. If I am burgled I need them to come and sort it out. But if they are racist to me I will tell them.'

The difference from the earlier debates on nuclear defence could not be more marked. Then the church had individual members who cared and wanted to make their views known. But there were different views. Individuals and groups of individual Christians could make an impact, but the church as a whole could only offer the confused sound of general universal care.

In the debate following the Stephen Lawrence affair when it was generally believed that a young black man had been killed in South London by white youths who got away with it because of police bungling in the 1990s, the church spoke with one voice. Neville Lawrence said: 'I think I understand how God feels because, although it was painful for me, maybe my son was sent to do something.'

The church has an opportunity to direct its prayers towards guiding its future statements and actions, speaking with one voice. It is not an opportunity it can miss.

Because the church is a body of compassion with a history of its members being put to death or imprisoned for their faith, the topic of prisons and prisoners is included in intercessions at regular intervals. We can pray especially for those who are falsely imprisoned (according to our understanding) throughout the world. The intensity of public prayer in parish churches for the safe release of Terry Waite, the Archbishop of Canterbury's special envoy, imprisoned while dealing with political hostages in the Middle East, was impressive. Undoubtedly the strength of this feeling expressed publicly in – but not only by – prayer was one of the pressures on the Foreign and Commonwealth Office encouraging their negotiations. (This was needed as some of the FCO felt that Terry Waite had acted against their advice in becoming involved in his last venture in that part of the world.)

As far as prison establishments in the UK are concerned, even though they have chaplains, and many active Christians are prison visitors, there is not the same contact as with hospitals and their chaplains. Perhaps there is a wish not to get involved with the remedial and educational work of prisons. One rarely gets the impression that parish congregations, though prepared to ask God through their intercessions to help prisoners, are active themselves in seeking out released prisoners and offering help. If they were then the Christian campaign to improve prison conditions would surely be more effective.

One of the issues on our own doorstep that comes up regularly in intercessions is Northern Ireland. It is a trouble spot and it is in the national news, so it gets included. Most congregations will pray with deep feeling for the victims of any outrage, terror or bombing. But they fight shy of expressing the fact, in prayer, that the conflicts in that part of the UK have a religious dimension. It is almost as if they just don't want to know or acknowledge that fact. When this came up at a meeting discussing intercessions in the parish where I worship one member said: 'I know that both the Protestants and the Roman Catholics say that they are Christians but they can't be real, proper Christians, can they, or they wouldn't be fighting one another.' This entirely ignores the fact that different factions, denominations, groups, etc. of Christians have been fighting and killing one another throughout history up to and including the present day.

The problem is not in the substance, but the image; not the reality but the perception. The non-Christian world does not understand. They look at the situation in Northern Ireland and ask, Is that what Christians are really like? How can they offer the rest of us either peace of mind, or peaceful living when they behave like that to each other? To stop pretending that there is not a religious aspect to the Northern Irish troubles is a Christian duty. The whole problem can then be put before God and those Christians working for reconciliation in the Province be supported practically and with understanding.

The church will bring before God those suffering from addiction: from drink or drugs, or whatever. But in seeking God's help the church is also becoming, through its network of local and national systems, a practical forum ready to take on debate about the nature of addiction and whether it is the substance itself or the personality of the person concerned that is the essential factor. Even though parts of the church are often criticized nowadays for not being 'relevant to youth', in my experience it is in countless, small groups throughout the country – young people in church halls – that the problem is actually being talked about, and making people think. Groups in the church are not campaigning to legalize any drugs, but they are providing a forum for people to question the morality of the different laws on drink and drugs, to look at the growing and serious crime situation in relation to drugs, and the impact the whole problem is having on gaps between different generations. It may well be that this church model of small discussion groups – if active Christians use their intelligence, sensitivity and influence – can be extended into the secular world.

One problem occasionally presented to God in intercessions, but not as often as non-Christians might expect, is the whole area of people's sexuality, gender and sexual orientation. This is a highly confused area for the church because it touches directly on the lives and functions of priests and puts the church at a disadvantage when dealing with the secular world. How can the church preach against discrimination and expect to be taken seriously when it has an entirely pragmatic and expedient policy with regard to women priests? Does anyone in the Church of England seriously think that it is God's will that women bishops are unacceptable, or that some parishes can be no-go areas for women priests? Change the word 'women' to 'black' and say that is the policy of the church and outrage and rebellion would occur. The sad thing is the church doesn't see how silly this attitude is and how it diminishes its effectiveness in campaigning for the rights of others. Nobody either in the church or out of it seriously thinks that this situation won't change over the coming years. It is just tough on the women currently affected by the position. Imagine a government department saying that to the church as a reason why the Government supports discrimination. The clergy would rightly be up in arms.

Over the issues of sexual orientation, the stance now seems to be that this is a matter for the church. On the whole, the secular world doesn't really care if priests are single, married, divorced or homosexual. Hopefully, part of the prayers directed to God seeking guidance on this issue will ask for help that the church seem neither too inward-looking nor ridiculous. I visited a marvellous 84-year-old man in hospital and heard a salutary comment: 'Why doesn't the church show the world they are far more concerned about how good someone is as a priest – not their sex life.'

The church could spend a lot of time praying and discussing its own procedures, views and attitudes, in both worship and witness. Some of this is probably inevitable. But Christians feel that there is a greater duty and a responsibility to bring before God those pertinent issues affecting his creation and to seek guidance on his will. Some issues occur regularly and are prayed for every Sunday, others come to the fore from time to time. Having presented these issues to God the Christian duty does not stop there.

9

Public Praying and Campaigning: Lobbying

As Christians we bring issues before God every Sunday in our intercessions. Some of these issues we feel strongly about. Do we not then have a duty, as the body of Christ on earth, to try to do something about these issues ourselves on all the other days of the week?

If we accept that we do, then we immediately have to deal with the question of not all Christians feeling or thinking the same way on the same issue. Though this is not always the case: often much good inter-denominational work is done, as in the case of Christian Aid, with the church moving forward as a whole. On some single-issue subjects, such as Sunday trading, there was, not surprisingly, almost complete agreement that the church would, as a body, oppose the measure. However, this is not true of most subjects. Lady Young, who led the campaign in the House of Lords to defeat the Labour Government's measure to reduce the age of consent for homosexual activity to sixteen, seemed surprised that while five bishops supported her, three voted against. She told the *Church of England Newspaper*, 'I am very sad about the state of the Church of England today. It would be nice if Christians spoke with one voice but they don't.' As a former Cabinet minister she should have known better. The idea that the church will speak with one voice on homosexuality – at the present time – flies in the face of experience. It is one of those many issues where, if you wish to participate in campaigning, a judgement must be made on how far to direct energies inside the structure of the church, and how far to do so outside.

As an individual Christian starting from scratch, to be effective in changing opinions in the secular world the first thing to decide is how far membership of the church is going to be useful to you. Let us consider one hypothetical, but classic, example of the 'Not in my back yard' type. You are keen to support the establishment of a half-way house for young offenders. It is planned for your parish. You feel that instinctively many of your friends at church will oppose the idea. You have to make a decision as to whether it is better to win them round to your point of view and gain support for the project, or keep quiet. If you alert them to the possibility and don't win them round they will organize opposition and the scheme might be defeated. In the case of this example it might be better not to use your connection with the church at all, while still following what you personally consider to be a Christian approach.

This can be identified as almost the first rule of lobbying. Any overt attempt to change opinion, and possibly legislation, is likely to produce an equal and opposite reaction to keep the status quo. This is an important consideration because governments – and other organizations – use this factor as a balancing agent. This is seen time and time again on such issues as fox-hunting, public schools and the Euro-currency. Some of the most successful changes in public life have come about extremely quietly. I refer to success being in the manner of change, not necessarily in substance. The lobby for the introduction of commercial television had almost completed its task before other people and organizations, including the Church of England, had realized what was up.

If as an individual with a mission you wish to gather a group of like-minded people around you, the starting-point is what appeals to them. You may want to work for a change in the taxation system. If you can slant that to show that it would benefit the institution of marriage you should be able to find a group inside the Church of England to help you. You may, as a Christian, feel that marriage should play a key part in the proposals for teaching 'citizenship'. As teaching this subject is now government policy you have an opportunity to use the groups and individuals inside the church that have an interface with government to be effective.

If the rule 'beware of stirring up opposition' is regarded as negative then the first positive rule is to decide the objective. Do you want to raise the matter for debate as a serious item of public interest which should be openly discussed, such as, say, the dangers of drink in society? Or do you want to take that a stage further and lobby for legislation for shorter opening hours for public houses? Bearing in mind the organized opposition that would bring it might be completely counter-productive to the first idea of merely having a public debate.

With a clear objective in mind, targets must then be identified.

There is no point in wasting time and effort in a campaign directed at the Government when the real power of decision-making lies with the local authority. In the same way, there is no point in going after a local authority if the real villain you want to take on is a regional planning authority, or the Tote, or a water company, or whatever. This often takes some research but it saves time in the long run and helps morale. There is nothing worse for a group of enthusiasts than to discover that they have spent their evenings addressing letters to the wrong people.

The best starting place for research is the public library. Our librarians are superb and very generous with their time. If you go to them and say, 'Look, this is what we want to do. Please can you help me find out who is responsible, or who the owners are, and what is their address', you will get a good response.

If the library fails, and they probably won't because if need be they will pass on your enquiry to a specialist library, then Members of Parliament are a marvellous free resource facility. A golden rule: on any matter where you need information you think the Government can supply, don't ask a government department yourself; go to your MP. Every letter to a minister from an MP has to be dealt with – if only by a holding letter – in ten days. Your local MP will help you; you are a constituent and your vote counts. All MPs see themselves as representing all the people in their constituency, irrespective of party allegiance or how they voted; in the same way a Church of England minister is a priest for all in the parish.

There are ways of approaching your MP which are more successful than others. Find out, through the public library, the local newspaper, or the telephone directory under 'Useful local numbers', when the MP's surgery is held. Ring the agent or secretary to make an appointment and send a short letter giving the gist of the matter you want to discuss. Do not write in green ink and do not write in the margins. That is regarded as a sure sign of a letter from a nutter and will not be given the attention you deserve. Write a letter of thanks afterwards. If your campaign is in any way directed towards the Government you will need the MP's help later on.

Having identified your target think carefully about how that target can be reached. If it is a government minister, find out what you can about what influences the minister's decisions. This is what commercial and industrial concerns do all the time and there are specialized companies who operate solely in the field of parliamentary and political public relations. But at whatever level the campaign is being fought, the basics of the operation are the same. You may not be able to pay a company to find out that one of the minister's interests is ballet and organize a charitable 'do' for her to attend (or even that her husband is a rugger fanatic and take him to Twickenham in the hope that they sometimes have conversations), but you can do research to find out something about how that minister operates.

Slowly build up a platform from which to be effective. It takes time and care. Everybody involved in this process must decide if they want to construct a permanent pressure group or organization, such as Oxfam, or Amnesty International; or are concerned with a single-issue project such as free access to cathedrals and museums. Christians then have to decide how far to work inside the church, using their influence on the machinery of church government, and how far to work outside the church, bearing in mind that some who will support the same ends might not like a close association with the church. Decisions must also be taken about how far inter-denominational approaches will be successful. On some matters, the different historic backgrounds of the Roman Catholic Church and the Methodist Church might result in more inward-looking argument than productive campaigning activity.

Probably a mixture of working for church involvement and with outside help will be needed, with the balance changing depending on the circumstances. As far as the Church of England is concerned if the General Synod, the Board of Social Responsibility and the bishops see that a campaign stimulated by Christian principles is gaining support (such as 'Crisis at Christmas') they will be more likely to get involved. Similarly if the government department that is being targeted sees that the Church of England is among supporters for the campaign, that may help. It will certainly help in that the church has access to the corridors of power.

Many Christians coming new to an activity which involves lobbying a minister will throw up their hands in despair and say it can't be done. Yes it can, but it does require directed thought and not just blind enthusiasm and belief in a cause. Generally speaking mass demonstrations are as ineffective as thousands of people sending the same letter to their MPs.

This is a case of back to basics. Lobbying, a term now used to cover all aspects of attempting to present a case to Government, is of American origin. It refers to those people paid by business in the USA to wait in the lobbies of the House of Representatives and the Senate to seize on politicians and present their case to them, often with the possibility of money changing hands. It led Mark Twain to write:

'The only definition of an honest politician is one who once bought, stays bought.' In the UK the term 'lobby' also refers to those parliamentary journalists with passes to the Palace of Westminster who go to official off-the-record meetings, and talk to Cabinet ministers and others to get background material which they publish without revealing their sources. There are overtones of secrecy in lobbying: when campaigners talk to ministers, at least one side, if not both, might prefer that it was off the record.

To those who say that this is all too ambitious and that their campaign would not get anywhere near coming to the attention of a minister, let me set this scenario. At local level if you did not know any chairs of council committees your parish priest probably would. He or she could intercede for you. At national level if your bishop does not have a seat in the House of Lords he will know a bishop who does. The point is that all Cabinet ministers of spending departments have junior ministers who sit just in front of the bishops in the House of Lords. So contact is possible. A line of contact from regular church attender via priest or church warden to bishop to junior minister is a possibility. Much campaigning is weighing up the various possibilities and then taking action. It may well be the line above would not work. There may well be lack of interest or goodwill; the chemistry of relationships may be bad. But it is a possible course of action; and you need many such courses.

It is important for all members of a campaigning group to be aware of their relative strengths and weaknesses. Some would hate approaching a bishop but be good at designing posters. Others could draft letters appealing to local radio but would not want to broadcast themselves. One or two would be happy beavering away in the reference section of the library, looking up the hobbies of Cabinet ministers in *Who's Who* in case there is a line there. One or two might like nothing better than being at Westminster talking to backbench MPs or visiting newspaper offices. It is horses for courses and in a successful operation all are made to feel of value.

In any approach to Government, MPs must be used. Do not worry if your MP is not particularly interested. MPs have a lot of conflicting pressures acting on them. They may not have power but they do have influence, and any number of competing people and causes want access to that influence. If the MP shows no signs of direct interest there are two courses of action. The first is to study the factors that interest him or her and see if there is a way through in any direction. There will be a variety of factors acting on an MP and having influence: ministers, other backbenchers, committee chairmen,

87

national party, local party, constituents, local and national media, consultancies, other pressure groups. There could be lots of long shots here. I know of one campaign that worked very strongly on regional whips, letting it be known that some sitting MPs were not really responding to the attentions of their constituents. The prospect of deselection concentrates the mind.

The other thing to do is to search the reference books and the internet to find those MPs who have similar interests to the aims of your campaign. If your own MP won't let you know then a list of MPs from *The Times Guide to the House of Commons* and a trawl through *Who's Who* will tell you which MPs have what interests. A look at *Vacher's Parliamentary Companion* will show which MPs sit on select committees, backbench party committees, and all-party interest groups. It is then easy to track down who has expertise in the areas of playgroups, or shopping malls, or disabled people, or mental health, or whatever. Once you find like-minded Members of Parliament who agree with your proposals your job is made a lot easier. They will have access to other national or international groups with the same concerns. They will know how to go about putting down Early Day Motions to gather the support of other MPs and when to ask parliamentary questions.

All this is building the platform so that jointly with friendly MPs you can approach junior ministers and then Cabinet ministers. It takes time and all campaigns suffer disappointments and setbacks, but it is possible.

Access is only the beginning. There is then the long haul of trying to get legislation through Parliament. In practice this means winning the hearts and minds of the governing party and having the technical help for Orders in Council or bills to be framed that make satisfactory progress through both Houses. But if your operation has got this far you will have on board relevant organizations and your supporting MPs will be guiding you through the civil service avenues.

As a long shot you may decide to spend time (and probably money) on drafting a bill in the hope that you can persuade an MP to take it through as a private member's bill. The first two MPs whose names are pulled out of the hat have a chance, with goodwill and time from the Government, to get an Act on to the statute-book. MPs who win the lottery are besieged by ready-made bills being pushed upon them, as if they had no thoughts of their own – which they often don't, entering the lottery in the same spirit one spends £1 on Saturdays, with no real thought of winning.

However, for airing the subject it is sometimes worth persuading an

MP to raise the issue at an adjournment debate at the end of the day; or in a Ten-Minute Rule Bill. Neither will achieve legislation but the Ten-Minute Debate may attract notice outside of the House.

If progress goes badly in the Commons remember that the Lords is much more relaxed and often peers are more approachable. Their interests too are listed in guide books and members of the new House of Lords will be delighted to find people searching for advice. They can't legislate but they can chivy.

Don't be disheartened if your local MP is an opposition member. Even if they haven't got a pairing arrangement with a member from the government party, Westminster is a fairly friendly place behind the scenes and they can normally operate the usual channels to find a helpful MP on the other side.

The campaign should not just be Westminster-based, even if the Government is the sole target. Governments are influenced by factors other than MPs at Westminster, especially the media. There are three approaches to be made to radio, television, newspapers and magazines. They all come with a word of warning. It may be important to use the media, but they have a different agenda to you. Once you give them your story, line and approach, they will not use it in the way you want, but in the way they want. They may put the stress on something other than what you want. One charity seeking press attention to back up an approach to ministers gave the papers a list of their patrons. One tabloid did some digging and found one of the titled patrons had not attended a meeting for a year. They did some more digging and discovered that wasn't the only charity to which the lady in question paid lip-service. They ran the story that certain charities took important people on board and then didn't use them. This is more likely to happen in the area of news, or features, rather than specialist comment. Probably the most useful journalists are those engaged in specialist reporting. They will welcome the chance to be introduced to new activity in their field – especially those who write for the trade press. A church campaign for certain ingredients to be part of 'citizenship' taught in schools would be written up in the trade press of the church, *The Church Times* or *Church of England Newspaper* for instance, as well as the trade press in education, the *Times Educational Supplement* for example. It would also attract the attention of the education correspondents of the broadsheets to the extent that they would welcome a meeting with leaders of the campaign and would study the literature being put out. Probably an item would appear under their by-line. To get into features in the papers, or merit a feature-type programme on radio or television, something of substance would be needed, perhaps tied to an item such as the rise of teenage pregnancies. The news pages might be interested in specific meetings with the leaders of the campaign and relevant ministers. Don't go to the wrong people with the wrong type of information. Find somebody among your supporters who is a journalist or has relevant experience in that field and be guided by them. If you don't know anybody who seems qualified go to the appropriate officer in the diocesan office. Most now keep lists of local Christians who have expertise which might come in handy.

There is a tangential point to be considered in the context of campaigns and the Church of England. Whatever corporate image the church wants to put across of itself is qualified by the fact that the image is the sum total of all Christians and the image they put across. The church may well use pop stars and sports personalities to give an exciting national image, and use posters of dead rebel leaders, but it is the local image that is much more immediate. In the same way that most constituents of a European constituency could not name their Member of the European Parliament (especially now we vote on a List system), so most people living in a diocese would not recognize or know the name of their bishop. But many local people tend to know their clergy by sight because they see the dog collar. That is from where much of their image of the church comes. In addition to any campaigns Christians undertake at either local or national level, all should be concerned with the continuing presentation of the church and Christianity at its most visible, that is, local level.

I O

Speeches and Sermons

THE spoken word is one of the most important weapons for both politician and priest. Everybody can become at least competent in speaking in public. Some can become outstanding. Winston Churchill maintained there were three basic rules to follow: study other speakers; don't copy them, but find a style and method which is personal to you; prepare.

Many people starting out and hoping for a career in politics or the church will say that they agree with that, but they still don't know where or how to start. This was advice given by Archbishop William Temple to Lancelot Fleming, later a bishop himself, which Fleming passed on to his clergy in Portsmouth. The starting-point, Fleming would tell his clergy, is that you are going to open your mouth and words are going to come out which must be heard by your audience. With a friend, take it in turns to read out loud from a book to each other in the largest room you can find. Adjust the level of your voice and the pace of your delivery until you can each hear clearly and without any strain what the other is saying. This is simply basic performance technique. Without being absolutely on top of that nothing else will follow. Yet it is amazing how often one hears in churches, both clergy and laity, and even MPs in the House of Commons, examples of those who have not bothered to master the art of clear delivery.

The next art to be considered is that of timing. For most speeches and sermons there will (thankfully, say many audiences) be a time limit. Normally, especially at the start of careers, the time will be given to the speaker by the organization they are to address. 'You can have ten minutes', or 'Half an hour plus questions', is the type of instruction given to the trainee cleric or MP. Generally the time limit has no relationship at all to the nature of the subject but relates to the programme planned for the occasion and how long the organizers think the audience can stand. In an ideal world it may well be that a speech on 'The State of the Nation' should command more time than 'Little-known Ways of Arranging Flowers'. But – from the speaker's point of view – the ideal world would not have an organist that plays too long and a matins service that starts at 11 o'clock, or a caretaker who wants to lock the hall before the pubs shut. The days when Gladstone spoke for thirteen hours are long gone.

It is an essential part of preparation to plan a talk into the allocated time. For this, go back to reading aloud from a book. Set a stopwatch or an alarm clock to go off after a minute. Just read out loud in a normal public-speaking voice until the pinger goes. Count the number of words you have read. In case it is an unusual text repeat this exercise three times and take the average number of words. For easy maths let's say that you find you speak out loud at the rate of 100 words a minute (in practice it will be more). If you have been asked to speak for ten minutes then you obviously need to prepare around 1000 words.

Remember that this is only a guide. When you speak there will be times when the subject matter requires you to pause for effect, or speed up or slow down the pace of delivery. Hopefully you may have breaks for applause, laughter – or even heckling (unlikely in church). But you now have the confidence of knowing how much material you need. For those who can't envisage what 1000 spoken words looks like think in terms of four sides of A4 paper covered with double-spaced typing.

This means that the speaker now has a time structure into which their words can be fitted. So if you wanted to divide a talk into three equal parts, on 'God – Father, Son and Holy Ghost', you would plan around 300 words on each, leaving 50 words for the introduction and 50 for the conclusion. Not that I am recommending anyone prepare a 1000-word script for a ten-minute talk and then read it out. But that basic preparation is as necessary for a good speaker as it is for a modern abstract artist to be able to draw still life.

As the speaker moves on to the next stage of getting the substance of the sermon or talk ready they will have in the back of their mind that the final product is going to be so many words, or so many sides of A4 paper. This provides a structure for self-discipline for research and making notes. You may be very keen to include a personal anecdote which puts you in a good light and you think will get a laugh, but that could take up to 15 per cent of your time. Does it add to what you want to say, or does it distort the balance?

Two great Conservative orators of this century, Enoch Powell and Iain Macleod, once shared a flat. They both developed the same way of preparing a speech. They would draw up two columns. In one they would put headings of all they actually knew about the topic. So if they were both doing a speech about 'Europe', one column would be labelled 'Know'. They might both write down: background; 1957 Treaty of Rome; enlargement; democratic accountability; taxation rates; farming etc. But in the next column, under 'Want to say', they would, given their different pro (Macleod) and anti (Powell) views, write different items: either, 'need to become a greater part of', or, 'need to withdraw'. Then, studying those two columns they would see where greater research was needed on their part.

This is a way of working anyone can follow at any level, and not just politician and priest. For example, you have been invited to make a speech presenting a farewell gift to a work colleague. In the list of what you know you write: current job, secretary of company cricket team, got best car parking space. Under 'Want to say', you put: great chap; wish well in developing hobbies in retirement; you know how much his family has supported him. Under 'Research', you put: find out – date joined firm, what hobbies actually are, details of family. Your research takes you to company records and conversations with close friends. It is the same research principle as using libraries, newspaper reports and the internet.

Having added research findings to your own original views you may then find that what you wanted to say isn't actually supported by the facts. There are two approaches to this situation. Either follow the example of orators through the ages and don't let the facts get in the way of fine words; or modify your approach. Whatever you do, you will now have too much material and the process of classification, sifting and rejection begins.

List all the points you want to make. Put similar points together and try to make a précis of them. List the group in what seems to be a sensible running order based on chronology and logical progression and then apportion minutes to each section. In a sermon on bereavement it may only be necessary to devote one minute to the resurrection because most of the congregation will understand what you mean. But the role of the undertakers in death may need more minutes as not all the congregation will have had second-hand experience of their work.

Keep the number of points you make down to the minimum. Though you worked hard at establishing a logical progression from A to Z most of the audience will not carry that progression away in their heads: 100 per cent of them will not be concentrating on your speech or sermon for 100 per cent of the time. The theme may well pass them by, but hopefully one or two well-presented points will stay in some of their minds to be recalled with usefulness at a later stage. Otherwise preaching is just self-indulgence. If you make seventeen points how likely are they to remember even a few? Stress three points and one might strike home.

The substance of the address is now dealt with and what follows concerns presentation and delivery – equally important and in need of thorough preparation. There is no point in having brilliant ideas to convey if people can't hear them or fall asleep through boredom. The substance has to be there before the presentation, otherwise the speech becomes meaningless froth. With the main body of the speech decided upon the next two things to be prepared are an opening and a conclusion.

The opening must be simple. There is a Westminster story – an urban political myth – which I have heard based on ten different MPs, which illustrates the dangers of trying to be too clever in opening remarks. A young newly adopted candidate asks his constituency chairman for advice. The chairman says, 'Why don't you do what I do. First of all shock your audience. Then, having got their attention, reassure them. Say, "It may surprise you to know that I am happy and indeed proud to stand before you today and freely admit that I have spent some of the happiest times of my life in the arms of another man's wife." Then pause, let it sink in and add, "I refer of course to my Mother".'

The candidate thought this good. He even thought he could enlarge it, so, getting to his feet he started off with great confidence, 'Ladies and Gentlemen, it may surprise you to know that even in these days of Tory sleaze (for he was a Conservative) I am very happy, indeed proud, to admit that I have been doing what all Tory MPs are expected to do. I have been spending ... (and here he lost the track, forgot his words, started to dry up and spoke more slowly and with hesitation) ... some of my most happiest times in the arms of another man's wife ... But ... I can't ... for the life of me ... remember who she was.' At which point the chairman hissed to him, 'It was your Mother, you fool. Your Mother.' 'Oh, yes,' said the candidate, pointing wildly at the chairman, 'I remember now. It was your Mother, wasn't it?' Collapse of all stout parties.

When you do find a good opening that works and suits you, refine it and hang on to it, for it can be used to different audiences over and over again. Roy Hattersley (now Lord Hattersley) developed an opening during the long years of Labour opposition up to 1997 which he finely honed and used to good effect many times, never using it in print, or on radio or television. Hattersley would get up to speak and say:

> Mr Chairman it is with a sense of considerable nostalgia that I rise to speak today. For it was in this very room . . . (name changes, depending on venue, at The Savoy, The Dorchester, whatever) that I made my first ever speech as a minister in Harold Wilson's Government. I was minister for consumer affairs and I was at an official lunch as chief guest of the Guild of British Tailors. It was quite obvious to me that many people in the room were not actually paid-up, card-carrying, members of the Labour Party and there was a certain resentment at the Guild having to deal with a Labour Government. Hoping to relax the atmosphere and defuse the situation a bit I said to the person sitting next to me – who was the Chairman of Aquascutum – look, I want to try and establish an easier atmosphere, do you mind if, when I get up to speak I say, 'It's not every day that one comes out to lunch and finds oneself sitting next to one's tailor?' The chairman of Aquascutum looked me straight in the eye and said, 'Roy, I don't mind in the slightest if you say that. So long as you make it crystal clear that what you're wearing is not one of our suits.'

It always gets a nice relaxed laugh and it has the great advantage of being adaptable. Find an opening like that and it gives you two minutes, as you are recounting the anecdote, to look around the room, size up the audience, and make what mental adjustments you need before getting into the body of your speech. Far better than starting off by shuffling papers and looking at your notes and not making eye contact.

Eye contact is all-important. There are too many speakers, a large number of them clergy I am afraid, who are so concerned with what they want to say that they forget about making contact with the audience. They read their words. Inevitably this means their eyes are looking down on to a script and not out to the congregation. All clergy charged with training curates and deacons should encourage them to have the confidence not just to read a prepared text but to relate with the people.

If you know the first few words off by heart then you can use eye-contact time wisely. Iain Macleod used to start with the top left hand corner of the room, and as he was speaking his eyes would move along the rows of the audience, moving from left to right; next row, right to left, and so on. By the time he reached the person in the front row in the far chair on the right he knew where in that room there were areas of warmth to which he could turn during his speech.

Closing a speech is often much more difficult than starting one. A grand peroration with flowery language, carefully rehearsed beforehand, will often seem quite inappropriate in the cold light of a church hall with ten people wondering why on earth they came. Keep it short and simple. By all means, if you think there is a possibility of mass enthusiasm, have a rousing rallying cry prepared, but also have an 'I have tried to put the important points to you. Thank you very much for listening to me' type of ending ready.

It will depend on the audience and how your speech, talk, address or sermon went over. That is for you to judge, and you can't judge it if you read a speech. A head bobbing up and down looking alternately at words on a lectern and audience faces can become a distraction. As can using the modern prompt screens where the speaker's head goes from side to side as though he or she were at Wimbledon watching tennis. The thing to do is to know your material thoroughly and then to have a few key words written in large letters on a card on the table in front of you. For those starting off in the business of public speaking who want to reach a reasonable level of competence I would suggest, for the first few sermons (or whatever), writing the whole speech out in full. Ten minutes: a thousand words. When written, go through paragraph by paragraph précising down to about ten key words – one for each hundred prepared. Apart from anything else this is an excellent way of getting to know your subject. As time goes by and your style and confidence develop you will find on most occasions this thoroughness is not necessary.

A good thought on confidence came from Cosmo Lang. Before becoming Archbishop of York, when a Fellow of Magdalen College, Oxford, he would tell students to remember, 'If you are not nervous, that is not natural and you probably won't be able to rise to the occasion. Most of the people in the audience will be thinking, "I'm glad it's not me; I hope he does well."'

Many speakers are worried about the use of humour and jokes. I think there are three points a speaker should ask about using a joke as an illustration:

- Does it fit in with my natural style?
- Is it appropriate for the occasion?
- Does it actually help the theme of my speech along?

If the answer is yes to all three, then go ahead, but do make it fit in. Note how past masters of after-dinner speaking such as Jeffrey Archer and David Frost always alter any jokes so that they are tailor-made for their audience by relevant personal and geographical references.

Public speaking is an essential tool for all politicians and priests. God's 'Word' has come down to us by speech and listening. Records have been written over the Christian centuries but the world has no actual record of anything that Jesus wrote – only of what he said. And the vast majority of verbal contact that both politician and priest have with their public is by the spoken and not the written word. That is why this form of communication is so important. To return to Winston Churchill's advice: study other speakers. Robert Kennedy once told Iain Macleod that he thought an important thing was to read poetry and to spend a few minutes with your favourite poet before making an important speech. All three Kennedy brothers loved Tennyson and Jack Kennedy found that if he spoke after reading some verses of Tennyson the whole matter of word-scanning and intonation slipped into place.

Politicians, including Churchill and Kennedy, often stray into the area of Christianity in their orations. This is what Jack Kennedy said in his inaugural address, 'The torch has been passed to a new generation of Americans' in Washington (January 1961):

> Man holds in his mortal hands the power to abolish all forms of human poverty ... and all forms of human life. Yet the same revolutionary belief for which our forebears fought is still at issue around the globe, the belief that the rights of man come not from the generosity of the state but from the hand of God ... Here on earth God's work must surely be our own.

And here is Winston Churchill in a radio broadcast on the BBC, 19 May 1940:

> Today is Trinity Sunday. Centuries ago words were written to be a call and a spur to the faithful servants of Truth and Justice: 'Arm yourselves and be ye men of valour, and be in readiness for the conflict; for it is better for us to perish in battle than to look upon the outrage of our nation and our altar. As the Will of God is in Heaven, even so let it be.'

When Christian leaders do get involved with political issues they often have to deal with vitriolic responses from politicians along the lines, 'It's your job to tell people the difference between right and wrong. When you can show people are taking notice of what you say and the crime rate is coming down then you have time to get involved in other things.' So perhaps when they do, it is because they really feel strongly about an issue and they take care to present a deeply thought out and well-argued case.

One of the most outstanding examples in this country, this century, was George Bell's attack in the House of Lords in 1944 on the Allied bombing of German towns. He was then Bishop of Chichester, and it was generally thought that the unpopularity from the establishment he received for his criticism was the key factor in him not becoming Archbishop. Extracts from this speech are included in the Appendix: 'Political Speeches by Religious Leaders'. It is worth studying for its careful construction, brick by brick, of the case Bell is putting against the Government. At every point he covers himself by acknowledging that the Nazis started the wholesale bombing of cities first; that industrial, military and government establishments in cities are legitimate targets; and that therefore some civilians are bound to be killed.

The substance of the Bishop of Chichester's case is contained in two specific examples, that of the bombing of the cities of Hamburg and Berlin, and the devastation caused to residential, cultural and religious areas. The rhetoric comes from the questioning manner of his address, asking publicly of the British Government:

'Do the Government understand ...?'
'Are they alive not only to ...?'
'How is it then ...?'
'Is it a matter for wonder ...?'
'How can there be ...?'
'How can the bombers ...?'
'Why is there this blindness ...?'
'Why is there this forgetfulness ...?'
'How can the War Cabinet ...?'
'How can they be blind ...?'
'How can they fail to realize ...?'

So many rhetorical questions in such a short speech. There were two reasons for this. Bell was not trying to make a construction speech; he was trying to get on the agenda the subject not of war aims, but of war tactics. A very difficult exercise; as those who offered comments on the war in the Balkans know. Every government will try to combat criticism on their war tactics by presenting the attacker as trying to undermine our troops. This is made more difficult by a spate of questions coming from a firm base. The Bishop was also on safe ground using rhetorical questions in the House of Lords. By convention, speeches are heard in silence and no one would attempt a reply. Care must be taken. Harold Wilson was not so lucky using a rhetorical question during the 1964 general election campaign at Plymouth. Asking a crowded meeting, 'And why do I stress the importance of the Royal Navy?' he paused for a fraction too long and got the reply shouted back, 'Because you're at Plymouth'.

The next speech I include in the appendix is also that of a church leader making comment on war. Robert Runcie, the Archbishop of Canterbury, in a sermon of thanksgiving for the outcome of the Falklands War at St Paul's Cathedral in July 1982 preached for reconciliation, 'Our neighbours are indeed like us'. In terms of rhetoric this was underplayed compared with Bishop Bell's speech. This was partly because it was a sermon in a church setting, not a speech in a parliamentary chamber. But also because, as a soldier who had been awarded the Military Cross in the Second World War, his actual presence meant there was less need for dramatic words. There is not one rhetorical question in the sermon. The Archbishop's strength comes from his experience of war and Christianity. He uses this authority to present choices to the nation.

These two different approaches, at different times, in different places, from different people, but both on the subject of war, underline how important it is to get the right horse for the right course. It is a lesson to all speakers: think of the total context in which you will be making your remarks.

Martin Luther King's setting for his 'I have a dream' speech in 1963 could not have been more different from either the House of Lords or St Paul's Cathedral. Nearly a quarter of a million Americans gathered at the Lincoln Memorial in Washington to listen to this highly charged and emotional appeal to end racial discrimination. This of course was many, many more than heard Runcie or Bell. There was one other crucial difference. All the audience, which was mostly black, was on the same side as Martin Luther King. He was articulating their views – in a way many of them couldn't – and they loved him for it. In return he repaid them with purple prose which he could never have got away with at a TUC meeting on a wet November night in Sunderland. Historically everyone refers to the speech as 'I Have a Dream', which was a phrase used nine times and drew great waves of chorus from the crowds. In fact the peroration was based on the line 'Let freedom ring' (see appendix), also used nine times at the end of the speech. This was a wonderfully crafted speech, owing much to Churchill. Churchill's 'We shall fight them on the beaches ...' being reflected in Luther King's 'Let freedom ring from the prodigious hilltops ... the mighty mountains ... the heightening Alleghenies ... the snowcapped Rockies ... the curvacious peaks ...'. Such a bond did King form with his audience that he could even make up new words such as 'curvacious' as he went along.

A different kind of oppressed people were addressed by Pope John Paul II in Poland in June 1983, from the battlements of the Jasna Gora monastery. I include this in the appendix because of all four speeches this most firmly bases the need for social justice in the responsibility of Christians to do the will of God. As with Martin Luther King, the Pope structures his speech around specific phrases. In this case, just one, the words 'I watch'. The whole speech is a classic example of how a speaker firmly identifies themselves with his or her audience, 'This call of the Polish youth with the Polish Pope'.

In all four speeches and/or sermons we see Christian leaders – a pope, an archbishop, a bishop and a Baptist pastor – putting into practice the feeling that those things they pray about must also be those things they bring to the secular world in efforts to find solutions. It is not only witness in practice, it also shows the world that Christians are trying to use the word of God to carry out his will. That is why it is important that all who attempt to use his word in speaking in public are as good as they can manage to be.

Appendix:
Political Speeches by Religious Leaders

GEORGE BELL, BISHOP OF CHICHESTER, TO THE HOUSE OF LORDS, 9 FEBRUARY 1944

Why is there this forgetfulness of ideals?

I turn to the situation in February 1944, and the terrific devastation by Bomber Command of German towns. I do not forget the Luftwaffe, or its tremendous bombing of Belgrade, Warsaw, Rotterdam, London, Portsmouth, Coventry, Canterbury and many other places of military, industrial and cultural importance. Hitler is a barbarian. There is no decent person on the Allied side who is likely to suggest that we should make him our pattern or attempt to be competitors in that market. It is clear enough that large scale bombing of enemy towns was begun by the Nazis. I am not arguing that point at all. The question with which I am concerned is this. Do the government understand the full force of what area bombardment is doing and is destroying now? Are they alive not only to the vastness of the material damage, much of which is irreparable, but also to the harvest they are laying up for the future relationships of the peoples of Europe as well as to its moral implications? The aim of Allied bombing from the air, said the Secretary of State for Air at Plymouth on 22 January, is to paralyse German war industry and transport. I recognise the legitimacy of concentrated attacks on industrial and military objectives, on airfields and air bases, in view especially of the coming Second Front. I fully realise that in attacks on centres of war industry and transport the killing of civilians when it is the result of bona-fide military action is inevitable. But there must be a fair balance between the means employed and the purpose achieved. To obliterate a whole town because certain portions contain military and industrial establishments is to reject the balance.

Let me take two crucial instances, Hamburg and Berlin. Hamburg has a population of between one and two million people. It contains targets of immense military and industrial importance. It also happens to be the most democratic town in Germany where the anti-Nazi opposition was the strongest. Injuries to civilians resulting from bona-fide attacks on particular objectives are legitimate according to International Law. But owing to the methods used the whole town is now a ruin. Unutterable destruction and devastation were wrought last autumn. On a very conservative estimate, according to the early German statistics, 28,000 people were killed. Never before in the history of air warfare was an attack of such weight and persistence carried out against a single industrial concentration. Practically all the buildings, cultural, military, residential, industrial, religious – including the famous University Library with its 800,000 volumes, of which three-quarters have perished – were razed to the ground.

Berlin, the capital of the Reich, is four times the size of Hamburg. The offices of the Government, the military, industrial war-making establishments in Berlin are a fair target. Injuries to civilians are inevitable. But up to date half Berlin has been destroyed, area by area, the residential and industrial proportions alike. Through the dropping of thousands of tons of bombs, including fire-phosphorus bombs, of extraordinary power, men and women have been lost, overwhelmed in the colossal tornado of smoke, blast and flame. It is said that 74,000 persons have been killed and that three million are already homeless. The policy is obliteration, openly acknowledged. This is not a justifiable act of war ...

How is it then that this wholesale destruction has come about? The answer is that it is the method used, the method of area bombing. The first outstanding raid of area bombing was, I believe, in the spring of 1942, directed against Lubeck, then against Rostock, followed by the thousand-bomber raid against Cologne at the end of May 1942. The point I want to bring home, because I doubt whether it is sufficiently realised, that it is no longer definite military and industrial objectives, which are the aims of the bombers, but the whole town, area by area, is plotted carefully out. This area is singled out and plastered on one night; that area is singled out and plastered on another night; a third, a fourth, a fifth area is singled out and plastered night after night, till, to use the language of the Chief of Bomber Command with regard to Berlin, the heart of Nazi Germany ceases to beat. How can there be discrimination in such matters when civilians, monuments, military objectives and industrial objectives all together form the target? How can the bombers aim at anything more than a great space when they see nothing and the bombing is blind? Is it a matter of wonder that anti-Nazis who long for help to overthrow Hitler are driven to despair. I have here a telegram, which I have communicated to the Foreign Office, sent to me on 27 December last by a well known anti-Nazi Christian leader who had to flee from Germany for his life long before the war. It was sent from Zurich, and puts what millions inside Germany must feel: 'Is it understood that the present situation gives us no sincere opportunity for appeal to people because one cannot but suspect effect of promising words on practically powerless population convinced by bombs and phosphor that their annihilation is resolved?'

If we wish to shorten the war, as we must, then let the Government speak a word of hope and encouragement both to the tortured millions of Europe and to those enemies of Hitler to whom in 1939 Mr Churchill referred as 'millions who stand aloof from the seething mass of criminality and corruption constituted by the Nazi Party machine'.

Why is there this blindness to the psychological side? Why is there this inability to reckon with the moral and spiritual facts? Why is there this forgetfulness of the ideals by which our cause is inspired? How can the War Cabinet fail to see that this progressive devastation of cities is threatening the roots of civilisation? How can they be blind to the harvest of even fiercer warring, the desolation, even in this country, to which the present destruction will inevitably lead when members of the War Cabinet have long passed to rest? How can they fail to realise that this is not the way to curb military aggression and end war? This is an extraordinarily solemn moment. What we do in war – which, after all, lasts a comparatively short time – affects the whole character of peace, which covers a much longer period. The sufferings of Europe, brought about by the demonic cruelty of Hitler and his Nazis, hardly imaginable to those in this country who for the last five years have not been out of this island or had intimate associations with Hitler's victims, are not to be healed by the use of power only, power exclusive and unlimited. The Allies stand for something greater than power. The chief name inscribed on our banner is 'law'. It is of supreme importance that we who, with our Allies, are the liberators of Europe should so use power that it is always under the control of law. It is because the bombing of enemy towns – this area bombing – raises this issue of power unlimited and exclusive that such immense importance is bound to attach to the policy and action of His Majesty's Government.

ROBERT RUNCIE MC, ARCHBISHOP OF CANTERBURY, ST PAUL'S CATHEDRAL, 26 JULY 1982

A Spirit which enlarges our compassion

Our hope as Christians is not fundamentally in man's naked goodwill and rationality. We believe that he can overcome the deadly selfishness of class or sect or race by discovering himself as a child of the universal God of love. When a man realises that he is a beloved child of the Creator of all, then he is ready to see his neighbours in the world as brothers and sisters. That is one reason why those who dare to interpret God's will must never claim for an asset for one nation or group rather than another. War springs from the love and loyalty which should be offered to God being applied to some God-substitute, one of the most dangerous being nationalism.

This is a dangerous world where evil is at work nourishing the mindless brutality which killed and maimed so many in this city last week (an IRA outrage). Sometimes, with the greatest reluctance, force is necessary to hold back the chaos which injustice and the irrational element in man threaten to make of the world. But having said that, not all is lost and there is hope. Even in the failure of war there are springs of hope. In that great war play by Shakespeare, Henry V says, 'There is some soul of goodness in things evil, men observingly distil it out.' People are mourning on both sides of this conflict. In our prayers we shall rightly remember those who are bereaved in our own country and the relations of the young Argentinian soldiers who were killed. Common sorrow could do something to unite those who were engaged in this struggle. A shared anguish can be a bridge of reconciliation. Our neighbours are indeed like us.

I have had an avalanche of letters and advice about this service. Some correspondents have asked, 'Why drag God in?' as if the intention was to wheel up God to endorse some particular policy or attitude rather than another. The purpose of prayer and of services like this is very different and there is hope for the world in the difference. In our prayers we come into the presence of the living God. We come with our very human emotions, pride in achievement and courage, grief at loss and waste. We come as we are and not just mouthing opinions and thanksgiving which the fashion of the moment judges acceptable ... The parent who comes mourning the loss of a son may find here consolation, but also a spirit which enlarges our compassion to include all those Argentinian parents who have lost sons.

Man without God finds it difficult to achieve this revolution inside himself. But talk of peace and reconciliation is just fanciful and theoretical unless we are prepared to undergo such a revolution. Many of the reports I have heard about the troops engaged in this war refer to moments when soldiers have been brought face to face with what is fundamental in life and have found new sources of strength and compassion even in the midst of conflict. Ironically, it has sometimes been those spectators who remained at home, whether supporters or opponents of the conflict, who continue to be most violent in their attitudes and untouched in their deepest selves.

Man without God is less than man. In meeting God, man is shown his failures and his lack of integrity, but he is also given strength to turn more and more of his life and actions into love for other men like himself. It is necessary to the continuance of life on this planet that more and more people make this discovery. We have been given the choice. Man possesses the power to obliterate himself, sacrificing the whole race on the altar of some God-substitute. Or he can choose life in partnership with God the Father of all. I believe that there is evidence that more and more people are waking up to the realisation that this crucial decision peers us in the face here and now.

Cathedrals and churches are always places into which we bring human experiences – birth, marriage, death, our flickering communion with God, our fragile relationships with each other, so that they may be deepened and directed by the spirit of Christ. Today we bring our mixture of thanksgiving, sorrows and aspirations for a better ordering of this world. Pray God that he may purify, enlarge and redirect these in the ways of his Kingdom of love and peace. Amen.

MARTIN LUTHER KING, BAPTIST PASTOR,
LINCOLN MEMORIAL, WASHINGTON DC,
28 AUGUST 1963

I have a dream

Five score years ago, a great American, in whose symbolic shadow we stand, signed the Emancipation Proclamation. This momentous decree came as a great beacon light of hope to millions of Negro slaves who had been seared in the flames of withering injustice. It came as a joyous daybreak to end the long night of captivity.

But one hundred years later, we must face the tragic fact that the Negro is still not free. One hundred years later, the life of the Negro is still sadly crippled by the manacles of segregation and the chains of discrimination. One hundred years later, the Negro lives on a lonely island of poverty in the midst of a vast ocean of material prosperity. One hundred years later, the Negro is still languished in the corners of American society and finds himself an exile in his own land. So we have come here today to dramatize an appalling condition.

In a sense we have come to our nation's Capital to cash a cheque. When the architects of our republic wrote the magnificent words of the Constitution and the Declaration of Independence, they were signing a promissory note to which every American was to fall heir. This note was a promise that all men would be guaranteed the unalienable rights of life, liberty, and the pursuit of happiness.

It is obvious today that America has defaulted on this promissory note insofar as her citizens of colour are concerned. Instead of honouring this sacred obligation, America has given the Negro people a bad cheque; a cheque which has come back marked, 'insufficient funds'. But we refuse to believe that the bank of justice is bankrupt. We refuse to believe that there are insufficient funds in the great vaults of opportunity of this nation ... So we have come to cash this cheque ...

Now, is the time to make real the promises of democracy. Now, is the time to rise from the dark and desolate valley of segregation to the sunlit path of racial justice. Now, is the time to open the doors of opportunity to all of God's children. Now, is the time to lift our nation from the quicksands of racial injustice to the solid rock of brotherhood. It would be fatal for the nation to overlook the urgency of the moment and to underestimate the determination of the Negro. This sweltering summer of the Negro's legitimate discontent will not pass until there is an invigorating autumn of freedom and equality. 1963 is not an end, but a beginning ...

I have a dream that one day this nation will rise up and live out the true meaning of its creed, 'We hold these truths to be self-evident; that all men are created equal.'

I have a dream that one day on the red hills of Georgia the sons of former slaves and the sons of former slaveowners will be able to sit down together at the table of brotherhood.

I have a dream that one day even the state of Mississippi, a desert state sweltering with the heat of injustice and oppression, will be transformed into an oasis of freedom and justice.

I have a dream that my four children will one day live in a nation where they will not be judged by the colour of their skin but by the content of their character.

I have a dream today.

I have a dream that one day the state of Alabama, whose governor's lips are presently dripping with words of interposition and nullification, will be transformed into a situation where little black boys and black girls will be able to join hands with little white boys and white girls and walk together as sisters and brothers.

I have a dream today.

I have a dream that one day every valley shall be exalted, every hill and mountain shall be made low, the rough places will be made plains, and the crooked places will be made straight, and the glory of the Lord shall be revealed, and all flesh shall see it together.

... And if America is to be a great nation this must become true. So let freedom ring from the prodigious hilltops of New Hampshire. Let freedom ring from the mighty mountains of New York. Let freedom ring from the heightening Alleghenies of Pennsylvania. Let freedom ring from the snowcapped Rockies of Colorado. Let freedom ring from the curvacious peaks of California. But not only that; let freedom ring from the Stone mountain of Georgia. Let freedom ring from Lookout Mountain of Tennessee. Let freedom ring from every hill and molehill of Mississippi. From every mountainside let freedom ring.

When we let freedom ring, when we let it ring from every village and every hamlet, from every state and every city, we will be able to speed up that day when all of God's children, black men and white men, Jews and Gentiles, Protestants and Catholics, will be able to join hands and sing in the words of the old Negro spiritual, 'Free at last! Free at last! Thank God Almighty, we are free at last.'

POPE JOHN PAUL II,
CZESTOCHOWA, POLAND, 18 JUNE 1983

I Watch!

Our Lady of Jasna Gora is the teacher of true love for all. And this is particularly important for you, dear young people. In you in fact, is decided that form of love which all of your life will have and, through you, human life on Polish soil: the matrimonial, family, social and national form – but also the priestly, religious and missionary one. Every life is determined and evaluated by the interior form of love. Tell me what you love, and I will tell you who you are.

I watch. How beautiful it is that this word is found in the call of Jasna Gora. It possesses a profound evangelical ancestry: Christ says many times: 'Watch' (Matthew 26:41). Perhaps also from the Gospel it passed into the tradition of scouting. In the call of Jasna Gora it is the essential element of the reply that we wish to give to the love by which we are surrounded in the sign of the Sacred Icon. The response to this love must be precisely the fact that I watch.

What does it mean, 'I watch'? It means that I make an effort to be a person with a conscience and I do not deform it; I call good and evil by name, and I do not blur them. I develop in myself what is good, and I seek to correct what is evil, by overcoming it in myself. This is a fundamental problem which can never be minimised or put on a secondary level. No. It is everywhere and always a matter of the first importance. Its importance is all the greater in proportion to the increase of circumstances which seem to favour our tolerance of evil and the fact that we easily excuse ourselves from this, especially if adults do so.

My dear friends, it is up to you to put a firm barrier against immorality, a barrier – I say – to those social vices which I will not here call by name but which you yourselves are perfectly aware of. You must demand this of yourselves even if others do not demand it of you. Historical experiences tell us how much the immorality of certain periods cost the whole nation. Today when we are fighting for the future form of our social life, remember that this form depends on what people will be like. Therefore, watch.

Christ said to the apostles, during his prayer in Gethsemane, 'Watch and pray that you may not enter temptation' (Matthew 26:41). 'I watch' also means, I see another. I do not close in on myself, in a narrow search for my own interests, my own judgments. 'I watch' means love of neighbour; it means fundamental interhuman solidarity.

Before the Mother of Jasna Gora I wish to give thanks for all the proofs of this solidarity which have been given by my compatriots, including Polish youth, in the difficult period of not many months ago. It would be difficult for me to enumerate here in all the forms of this solicitude which surrounded those who were interned, imprisoned, dismissed from work, and also their families. You know this better than I. I received only sporadic news about it. May this good thing, which appeared in so many places and so many ways, never cease on Polish soil. May there be a constant of that, 'I watch' call of Jasna Gora, which is a response to the presence of the Mother of Christ in the great family of Poles. 'I watch' also means I feel responsible for this great common inheritance whose name is Poland. This name defines us all. This name obliges us. This name costs us all. Perhaps at times we envy the French, the Germans or the Americans because their name is not tied to such a historical price and because they are so easily free: while our Polish freedom costs so much ...

A nation then is first of all rich in its people. Rich in man. Rich in youth. Rich in every individual who watches in the name of truth: it is truth, in fact, that gives form to love.

My dear young friends. Before our common Mother and the Queen of our hearts, I desire finally to say to you that she knows your sufferings, your difficult youth, your sense of injustice and humiliation, the lack of prospects for the future that is so often felt, perhaps the temptations to flee to some other world. Even if I am not among you every day, as was the case in the past, nevertheless, in my heart I carry a great solicitude. A great enormous solicitude. A solicitude for you. Precisely because on you depends tomorrow. I pray for you every day.

It is good that we are here together at the hour of the call of Jasna Gora. In the midst of the trials of the present time, in the midst of the trial through which your generation is passing, this call of the millennium continues to be a programme. In it is contained a fundamental way out. Because the way out in whatever dimension – economic, social, political – must happen first in man. Man cannot remain with no way out.

Mother of Jasna Gora, you who have been given to us by Providence for the defence of the Polish nation, accept this evening this call of the Polish youth together with the Polish Pope, and help us preserve in hope. Amen.

11

Christianity and the British

THE 1998 Lambeth Conference held at the University of Kent caused more than a ripple of disquiet among British Christians. The periodically held international Lambeth Conferences are a calling together of all the bishops of the Anglican Communion under the Archbishop of Canterbury, for prayer, worship and discussion. It is the result of the world-wide growth of the Anglican Church which went hand in hand with Britain's colonial expansion. The process of decolonization has obviously led to different styles of development of the various 'provinces' and although the Archbishop is recognized as head the leadership is now local and not white, middle-class, male and British. It was the stand that some of the African bishops took on homosexuality that shook the British. To view homosexuality as a sin was regarded as one priest put it – not with great tact, but with great effect – as a real step back to the dark ages.

As the ripple spread outwards two questions were asked. The first was is there actually something about the tolerance of the Church of England as opposed to the whole Anglican community which means that we have to look again at the question posed by Canon Max Warren, former General Secretary of the Church Missionary Society (*The English Church: A New Look*) as to whether or not the Church of England is, in his words, 'fit for export'? Certainly, a direct result of that conference was that many Christians in this country now regard themselves as members of the Church of England rather than identifying with the wider Anglican Church.

To many this was a step backwards because it reinforced the idea that when it came to discrimination the church picked and chose according to whim. Women, homosexuals, divorcees – not only was there discrimination but there was a different scale of discrimination for clergy and laity, with the church condoning different standards of behaviour in different situations. What made it worse was the way the problem was entirely ring-fenced inside the church. The Rev. Alison Leigh, one of the first ordained women priests in 1994, now a priest-in-charge in a Kent parish, says: 'Outside the immediate church family people couldn't see what all the fuss was about.' The Rev. Anne Dyer, a Diocesan Ministry Development Officer, wrote in her diocesan newspaper: 'I have never had any problem being received as a priest by people outside the church.'

The church has always been selective about which causes to support in matters of discrimination. A shrewd observer on Christianity, Rabbi Lionel Blue, always asks why it took so long for Christianity to take a stand against slavery. If the Christian of today looks to the Bible for guidance, they will find, as William Wilberforce did, the Book of Philemon one of the oddest in the New Testament. So, it was ever thus.

But, in spite of the contortions of the Church of England, there has developed over the Christian centuries in this country a strand of Christian tolerance. Often the Church of England has had to go into contortions – and often charged with hypocrisy – to work with, if not to completely embrace that tolerance.

The stand taken by some of the African bishops at the Lambeth Conference which forced many members of the Church of England to consider their positions came just at a time when changing political and constitutional developments were leading to public debate in the media as to what it meant to be 'English'. One caller to a phone-in radio programme stumped the presenter with the genuine enquiry: 'Scotland is a Kingdom; Wales is a Principality; Northern Ireland is a Province – but what do we call England?'

What it means to be English obviously has great significance for members of the Church of England. It is difficult to be a satisfactory member 'of' something, unless you know what that 'of' stands for.

Probing in this direction for satisfactory answers is like trying to catch the proverbial straws in the wind. We have given the world its major language, and the Book of Common Prayer, and Shakespeare. But, unlike most other countries in the world, including the others in the United Kingdom, we have no national dress. We have no public holiday to celebrate our Patron Saint. Indeed in 1999, when an English landlady of a public house asked for an extension of opening hours for St George's Day, the magistrates refused on the grounds that 'it was not a special occasion'.

An examination of 'Englishness' and a study of the development of the Church of England feed off each other. The Church of England is

'English' because there are strands of national life and character which affect our church as much as there are strands of national life and character which affect the South American churches, the Bible-belt Christianity of middle America or the Roman Catholic churches of the south of France.

But also, 'English' culture and behaviour has been overwhelmingly affected by the spread of Christianity through the churches and especially since the Reformation through the Church of England. This is a factor which the church does not always recognize in its relationship with the secular world. We are all to a large extent children of our history. When that cultural history has such a predominate element of Christianity in it, the church – if it can harness the right intelligence and resources to use it – has an obvious starting-point for (in its broadest sense) mission.

To illustrate that consider the opening paragraphs of a highly effective piece written by the Editor of the *Daily Telegraph*, Charles Moore, on 23 April 1999:

Let us suppose your name is Mary and you are married to a man called John. You live in St. Albans. Each day you take a train to London and arrive at Blackfriars. From there you enter the Tube station and insert into a machine coins which say on them, among other things, 'D.G.Reg F.D.' and buy a ticket to St. Paul's where you work. You probably won't notice it, but every one of the details I have just described has a Christian reference – and it is still only 8.30 in the morning of your daily life.

Mary was the Mother of Jesus. John was the forerunner of Jesus. St. Alban was an early martyr. The Blackfriars are the religious order established by St. Dominic. When the hymn says, 'Brothers we are treading where the saints have trod', it is literally true. The abbreviations on our coins mean that the Queen is Queen by the Grace of God and that she is Defender of the Faith (a title conferred on Henry VIII by the Pope before things turned nasty). St Paul was the first and greatest bringer of Christianity to the Gentiles.

We even time ourselves from the date (or rather the somewhat inaccurate supposed date) of the birth of Jesus. The years and centuries count backwards from that time to whenever it was that the world came into being, and forwards from that time until today. They are either, 'Before Christ' or 'Anno Domini' (in the year of Our Lord.) We are just about to mark two millenniums of them. We shall soon enter 2000 A.D.

As everyone knows there is confusion and controversy about how to celebrate this moment. First came Michael (the name of the Archangel) Heseltine with the idea of a Dome, built by Richard (the name of a

Saint from Chichester) Rogers. Then this was backed by Anthony (of Padua?) Blair who gave the task to Peter (the apostle to whom Jesus gave the keys of the Kingdom) Mandelson, who sadly had to relinquish it and passed it on to Charles (the great Christian emperor) Falconer. It will be opened by Elizabeth II who takes her name from the mother of John the Baptist.

The points Charles Moore makes can be both multiplied and added to in great measure. The overwhelming number of the population, even in a growing multiracial society, and allowing for the spread of Kylies and Darrens, have 'Christian' forenames – over 30 per cent having been baptized in church. Over 250 towns and major villages in the UK are named after saints, from the delightful St Abbs in the Borders, to St Weonards in the Welsh Marches. In the *London A–Z* there are columns of streets listed after saints, from St Agatha's Drive in Kingston to St Winifred's Close in Chigwell. The streets of London also keep alive the names of saints such as Maur, Loo, Elmo and Erkenwald – who would otherwise long since have been forgotten. There are 31 'Trinities' in the *A–Z*. Our Christianity is all around us even as we walk to work or school or the shops.

It is ubiquitous, pervading, and up to date. Collecting for Christian Aid recently in an area full of new housing blocks I found two where the numbering on the doors went 11, 12, 12a, 14. The unlucky thirteen may be dying out as a number of people to avoid at a dinner party but it is still there in the minds of local authority planning officers. The presence of Judas, the thirteenth disciple, haunts us 2000 years on.

The cultural mores of Christianity affect us in so many ways. The threefold aspect of the Trinity has probably had a deep effect on our nature to split life into threes: every essay must have a beginning, a middle and an end; the day is divided into morning, afternoon and evening; the school and university terms are split into three.

Schools and universities have chaplains; so do hospitals and prisons. The Christian reminder is present at so many different levels and in so many different places. Not least in the arts, in particular literature, painting and architecture. It is not possible to walk around any major public art gallery in the UK without being aware of the effect that the Christian story has had on painters, curators and, because we look and think, on us.

In so many places the church is still the focal point – in a visible sense – the centre of the community. Towards the end of his life Dennis Potter said that though he wasn't a Christian he got an enormous feeling of uplift when driving into a town or village and seeing the church tower or steeple rising above the other buildings and thinking of the time and effort and talent and inspiration that people of that community had put into the building.

The elements of Christianity in our subconscious are great. People who are not Christians, who don't go to church, and who if questioned say that they don't believe, nevertheless still swear (as do many Christians!) 'Oh, my God' instinctively. The Rev. Mel Griffiths, a priest from Helmsdale in Sutherland, has collected a 1300-signature petition of complaint about the blasphemous references on the BBC's television programme *Changing Rooms*. He says: 'The BBC is abusing the name of God and *Changing Rooms* is by far the worst. I have to keep flicking over the channels to avoid the blasphemy.' I am afraid he will have to keep flicking. The words 'Oh, my God' are part of the Christian hinterland, which has entered our human psyche.

In many areas the presence of conscious Christianity is a deliberate choice by nation and church. Sometimes the initiative is taken by the church, sometimes by the state or a secular body. Sometimes this is formal; sometimes informal. For many years the English cricket team had a chaplain who was one of the few people with access to the players' dressing rooms. But though sanctioned by a bishop this was an informal arrangement, not to be found in any reference book.

In *Future Church*, Peter Brierley writes:

> The UK Anglican Church, like all other institutional Churches in the U.K. has seen decline in recent years – though not as sharp as, for instance, attendance at football matches or membership of trades union. But the hinterland around every Anglican Church is still full of nominal Anglicans, who are fundamentally well-disposed to the Church of England. How can we reach out to them to tap this fund of goodwill?

One way is an extension of what the church has often done: to go to people where they are. This is easiest with a captive audience, and chaplains in schools, colleges, hospitals and prisons play a notable part in what in the 1990s' jargon is described as 'outreach'. HM Prison Wormwood Scrubs uses a special prison Eucharist, the prayers of which a friend of mine who was a prisoner there found particularly helpful:

> Early in the morning
> surrounded by respectable liars,
> religious leaders, anxious statesmen and silent friends,
> you accepted the penalty for doing good,
> for being God:
> you shouldered and suffered the cross . . .

We have longed for a place to hide,
a place to avoid the risk of exposure.
But your light reveals our hiding place.
You search for us persistently, pervasively
until we are found.

It is probably in the armed services that the 'outreach' of Christianity is seen at its most public. The role of chaplains in warfare is one of historic importance in trying to bring salvation, in all the meanings of the word, to those in trouble. Both the two world wars, and all the other conflicts this century, record outstanding acts of Christian duty by some extremely remarkable men. There are lessons to be learnt from the books and papers left by these clergy. Douglas Winnifrith, a chaplain to an infantry brigade, wrote a book about his experiences in France in 1915 (*The Church in the Fighting Line*). He was killed in 1917. He wrote movingly of burying the dead under enemy fire and administering to the sick. Of conducting services in the field, he wrote:

> A great earnestness seemed to pervade one's congregation; how could it well have been otherwise, surrounded as we were by death and destruction? The services which, perhaps, impressed me as much as any were those conducted for the men in the billets. They would crowd in and sit upon the floor, and one was able to give them a straight heart-to-heart talk in a way that is not possible at a more formal service. It was then that the men would unburden themselves, produce from their pockets a New Testament, or some small book of devotions, from which they said they had derived much comfort and help, and speak of their Sunday School and choir-boy days. I have found few upon whom religion has not taken a strong hold, though ordinarily, they do not speak of it.

It was an army chaplain who put the story of Abraham and Isaac into context for me by explaining that the natural culture of the time meant that of course Abraham would put the sacrifice of his son to God before everything else; in the same way, in the First World War, parents expected their sons to answer the call of duty, even if that meant their sacrifice. It was the mood of the times, and we all cannot help but be creatures of our own times.

The church has had some success with industrial chaplains, and increasingly some city companies, businesses and retail outlets such as Marks & Spencer have a chaplain on a retainer, though sometimes in an honorary capacity, available to talk with their employees. This is simply turning on its head the idea of the priest being 'at home' either literally or in the church to talk to people: the clergy, and where appropriate laity, make themselves available where the people are.

This can work well in towns and cities where churches may work together to establish a drop-in centre. This would not be in church, because that can be off-putting for those not familiar with churches, but perhaps in rented shop premises in the High Street. It is more difficult in rural parts and there has been a feeling in parts of the Church of England that, unlike pre-war, the countryside is being neglected by the authorities who are too busy dealing with either the growing evangelical congregations or the problems of urban areas, to devote much attention to dwindling country parishes where one vicar looks after several churches.

In his book *Friends in High Places*, Jeremy Paxman writes:

> Country parishes have been low on the Church of England's list of priorities, starved of vicars and money, on the grounds that since Britain is largely an urban nation they have a less urgent call upon the Church's resources. The most dramatic social initiative of the Church in the eighties, *Faith in the City*, focused on the specific problems of inner cities. A later report on the difficulties of country parishes was commissioned only as an afterthought and owed its existence to the fact that the Archbishop of Canterbury was an amateur pig-breeder. The Duke of Westminster ran into the Archbishop while he was exhibiting his sows at the Royal Show and over tea offered to put up £100,000 to pay for the report.

Paxman quotes the Rev. Henry Thorold from Lincolnshire on the reasons for the shortage of clergy in the countryside:

> What about the crisis in the countryside? Why did this parish have no priest for six years? Shortage? Shortage? If there is it's because the Church is spending on bureaucrats. I met a former pupil of mine recently. Impressive young man. He'd become a clerk in Holy Orders. I asked him what he was doing. He told me he was a diocesan education officer, whatever that is. He'd no parish, you see. That's what the Church is spending money on, and that's why – all these canons and others with no proper job – they haven't got any parish priests.

In many ways this a parody. But in all parodies there is some truth, and this expresses the views some people have of the church. The 'Englishness' of the church gives a direct relationship with the people; it can also cause problems. The 'Englishness' of the church as built up in the fictional media, especially film and television, is a picture which has gone largely unchallenged by the establishment of the church. On the whole we do not see on our screens the clergy comforting the dying or wrestling with problems of theology. At the very best they appear as ordinary people as in *EastEnders* or, on radio, *The Archers*. In *The Vicar of Dibley* the woman priest is played with great sympathy and it is extremely funny. I am sure it has helped the cause of women priests. It is right that priests should be portrayed as ordinary people, but there is something missing – the role of priests in serious dramatic fiction. The clergy portrayed in the soaps are unexceptional and there is much to be said for showing that side of the clergy. But the characterization does not rise from that level – at worst it does sink below. Bernard Levin once wrote that one of the real media problems the church had was that the word 'vicars' rhymed with 'knickers'. So often the vicar is presented as a bumbling, well-meaning old fool who gets into worldly troubles with which he can't cope. The phrase, 'More tea, Vicar?' has entered into the language as shorthand for comfortable suburbia.

The church still has a lot to come to terms with in its relationship with the media; both working behind the scenes over a long period to change the fictional image of clergy, and also knowing how to respond when one of its real-life clergy finds themselves in trouble with the tabloids. This is nothing that can't be done. One just gets the impression that the church hasn't yet put its mind to addressing problems in these areas.

At the turn of the century, Mandell Creighton, Bishop of London, declared, 'I am not ashamed to own that I am an Englishman first and a Churchman afterwards.' The intertwining of church and state means that as the ripples of Christianity spread outwards from the church an increasing number of people are affected because most in our English culture have some residual of Christian contact. There is the hard core who worship every Sunday – and their relations and friends. There are those who use the church at specific times in their lives for baptism, weddings or arranging funerals. There are those who turn automatically to the church – as though recalling some seemingly forgotten message – in times of sorrow, either individual or national. The many detailed links with Christianity in our day-to-day lives, as expressed by Charles Moore in his article in the *Daily Telegraph*, are also forged by the historic link between church and state in our collective psyche. In *Like a Mighty Army*, M. A. P. Wood compares this favourably with the situation in the United States, and talks about the unique English situation:

Because the visiting opportunities that one has in a parish are unique in the English situation they must be exploited for the Gospel. In America, for instance, no one has the right to knock on every door and call indiscriminately and the Episcopalian clergyman would be out of order if he did so. In England, however, the people have a semiconscious feeling that the Church of England ought to be interested and concerned for their well-being.

'A semiconscious feeling that the Church of England ought to be ... concerned for their well-being' – that feeling comes from the culture of Christianity that is deep in our society and it offers a wonderful chance for the church to be effective. Sir Timothy Hoare, a long-time member of the Standing Committee of the General Synod, member of the Chadwick Commission on Church and State, and a key member of the Church Youth Fellowships Association, echoes the words of many commentators when he writes in *Hope for the Church of England: Established to Serve the Nation*, 'Christianity remains the principal source of moral and ethical guidance for the nation.'

12

Other Ways: Denominations and Faiths

THERE are some parish churches where the traditional concept of 'Englishness' would hardly be recognized. In parts of our inner cities there has been revival of worship often with strong charismatic and/or evangelical overtones. But on the whole, though in many localities this has had a great impact on the parish it has hardly touched the national character of the Church of England – as any observer of the General Synod will testify.

There are many different ways of worshipping under the umbrella of the Church of England. This sometimes causes spats. I have witnessed arguments about religion between 'low' church and 'high' church members which makes one wonder whether they do actually belong in the same embrace. But, of course, we are much more likely to get involved in arguments with members of our own church than we are with members of another faith. Going to an interfaith conference once a conversation was going on in the back seat of my car which went like this:

> *'High' church member*: 'I don't understand how you can think that you suddenly experience a blinding light and then your life has changed for ever. We are all sinners. We are always going to sin. We just have to pray that our religion helps us cope with sinning.'
>
> *'Low' church member*: 'I don't know why you aren't a Roman Catholic. Have a sin. Go to confession. Have another sin. Go again.'
>
> *'High' church member*: 'I do go to confession. It's like having a bath. Do you have one to get clean? Or always have them to keep clean?' ... And so on.

Later that day they both had tea with a charming Indian and discussed arranged marriages. Instead of saying that such a concept would be totally alien to Christianity, they politely said, 'Ah, well. Yes. Well we do have a very high divorce rate in the UK.'

In many areas, both geographically and theologically, the different denominations of Christianity in the UK are coming together. But those who argue that greater unity must be a good thing and that all sides are slow in compromising have to remember the context. The Reformation is still a huge stumbling block. This was a far more fundamental schism than that between Rome and Orthodoxy and so many cultural, industrial and social factors have flowed from it to affect the development of Europe that some major recognition is needed. Without that unity with the Roman Catholic Church ecumenism may get trapped at local level. Pope John Paul II has already shown great pontifical humility by apologizing for the past persecutions by the church. Perhaps the millennium would be an appropriate time to reconsider the position of Martin Luther. Otherwise while there can be displays of unity on the surface, the great gulf on matters such as individual conscience, abortion, or the role of women in the service of Christ, are never going to be resolved. The significance is that it hampers the impact the church has on the secular world. Blatantly, Christendom says something to the world. The world responds by saying, in effect, why should we take you seriously: we have enough people telling us what to think, governments, newspapers, etc.; you can't even agree on your own subject.

The same model applies to politics and politicians. If different members of the Christian family argue amongst themselves, both inside and outside the same denomination, so do politicians. Most politicians are much nastier to, and about, members of their own party than they are about members of opposing parties. And it has the same effect on the general public as Christians squabbling among themselves. It turns them off. There is now so much pressure on people to get their attention that the average person who is not all that interested in the minutiae of religion or the details of politics is liable to say, 'Oh, Christians, they are all the same. They can't agree on anything. Always arguing among themselves.' They also (again apart from a few) will say, 'Oh, politicians. They are all the same. Always arguing among themselves. Why should we listen to them. Let's get on with life.'

For those Christians who work hard at establishing ecumenism, the sociologist Bryan Wilson has a disturbing observation. He maintains that when organizations want to link up with other similar organizations it is because they are weak. This certainly applies in politics. It is always the small third party that is keener to join a pact with a larger one to gain influence. In the 1950s the Conservatives and Liberals had a pact in many constituencies where one of them wouldn't put a candidate up so as to give the other a clear run against Labour. In the 1970s a weak Labour Government joined up with David Steel's Liberal Party to form a Lib-Lab pact to stay in power. The weak third party also benefited by having a more effective say in legislation. Before the 1997 general election Tony Blair was talking with the Leader of the Liberal Democrats, Paddy Ashdown, about the possibility of some kind of coalition after the election. When the Labour Party won such a massive majority that idea melted away like snow in spring, and the Liberal Democrats had to be satisfied with places in a Cabinet committee. In Scotland in 1999, after the elections for the first Assembly for over 300 years, no party had a clear majority so the Scottish Labour Party did a deal with the Scottish Liberal Democrats to form a coalition. They didn't come together in London because the Labour Party was strong. They came together in Scotland because the Labour Party was weak.

Can the same be true of the church? In the summer of 1982 the Pope preached alongside the Archbishop of Canterbury in Canterbury Cathedral. This would not have happened even twenty years earlier. Is it a sign of churches recognizing their weakness in a secular world and coming together to overcome that? Or is it a true sign that basic differences are being resolved? Wilson argues that, as with political parties, ecumenism is not popular when churches themselves are strong. Certainly one hears little of the spirit of ecumenism coming from the strong and growing Anglican churches of Uganda and Nigeria.

Working with the Methodist and Free Churches has always been easier for the Church of England. Some Methodists regard themselves as members of the Church of England, though the controversy over gambling and drinking is still apparent, as witnessed by the flurry of letters in the national press when it was suggested that Methodists take a slightly more tolerant attitude in the run up to the millennium.

The fundamental religious difference between Christians and those of other faiths is on the question of whether salvation is only possible through Christ. This is something that Christians themselves can't agree on – but heaven help the clergy who say that from the pulpit. Years ago it was all so simple. First of all Christians fought each other (they still do in some parts of the world). Then Protestants and Roman Catholics tried to find the things that united them. But they still went on missions to convert those of other faiths. Then they started thinking, if some common unity can be found between the various denominations of the same faith then surely there must be common ground – somewhere – among the various faiths. The stumbling block for Christians – in many cases not even a stumbling, just a block – was 'No one comes to the Father except by me' (John 14:6). Many attempts are being made to negotiate what would seem to be not negotiable. Some are textual attempts. In *Pray, Love, Remember*, Michael Mayne, formerly Dean of Westminster Abbey, writes, following the Multi-Faith Observance Service held at the Abbey on Commonwealth Day, 1994:

> Although the Observance is attended by Leaders of all Christian traditions, there was explicit and noisy criticism by a faction of the Church and a protest was sent to the Queen (Defender of the Faith). Much was made by our critics of Jesus' words, 'No one comes to the Father, except by me.' Yet that text relates specifically to the fatherhood of God: it is not simply a question of coming 'to God' but of coming 'to the Father'. There is but one God, in whom we live and move and have our being, and when we worship we stand before the mystery of the deep and eternal Reality to whom we give different names. From Jews we learn of His faithfulness: from Muslims of His sovereignty and mercy; from the wonders of the natural world a realisation of His mystery and power. Christians speak of something more intimate; of His fatherhood, for only in Jesus can we begin to experience the truth of God as Father. The presence of those from the Commonwealth of other faiths, each person praying to God as that faith conceives him to be, did nothing to compromise our belief that in Jesus Christ we see the ultimate expression of God's nature, for that belief does not deny the truth of other revelations of God, nor our hope that in Christ all may ultimately find their fulfilment.

George Carey, the Archbishop of Canterbury, has set a realistic lead in this matter. In over twenty speeches in the last decade of the twentieth century he has argued that while proclaiming and acting out our own firm belief in Jesus Christ as Lord we should avoid deliberate confrontation with those of other faiths. In the Morrell Address on Toleration, which he gave at the University of York, on 22 November 1991, he declared that to challenge other people's faiths would be both morally wrong, and counter-productive. He said: 'A predominately Christian society nurtures tolerance and constructive relationships with minority faiths in combating the shallow materialism of much contemporary life, and working together on matters of common concern, such as racism.' On another occasion he went on to say:

'Other faith communities enjoy freedom of worship, of association in this country, and if they wish they may evangelise. We hope for the same freedoms for Christians in lands where they are in a minority.'

In 1998 the Archbishop co-chaired the World Faiths and Development Dialogue at Lambeth Palace, with James Wolfensohn, President of The World Bank. Debate took place between the following participating international faiths: Bahai, Buddhist, Christian, Hindu, Jain, Jewish, Muslim, Sikh and Taoist. The discussion and prayers were not just about matters of religion, but spread across many areas of common concern. Here were religious leaders, in the case of the UK, priests, tabling an international agenda with, it can be argued, as much authority as politicians at the United Nations. The ripple effect may well be greater. Religious leaders return to their homes and the thoughts from their meetings spread outwards, of course slowly, and some with spin put on, but reach down to their followers. There is no great media attention, but perhaps over the years it is more effective as a way of spreading goodwill than the views of politicians spreading outwards from the United Nations. The politicians' views get as little attention from the media, but what they lack, which religions have, is a structure of world-wide membership, able to receive the leaders' messages.

This must be kept in proportion. Estimates tend to be guesstimates, but most surveys and reference books tend to agree that roughly 75 per cent of the world's population have some kind of religious affiliation, no matter how nominal. The largest religions do not necessarily have the greatest effect on world culture, though they may have a tremendous impact on the spirituality of individuals. For instance, Judaism has around 20 million adherents (0.3 per cent of the world's population) but it has had an international impact far greater than that of, say, the Chinese folk religions such as Taoism, which numbers 150 million followers.

The proportions of the world's population following the major different religions is given below. Because some people follow more than one religion, notably the Japanese, some of whom practise both Buddhism and Shintoism, the totals come to more than 100 per cent.

Christianity		33%
Roman Catholic	19%	
Protestant (excluding Anglican)	7%	
Orthodox	3%	
Anglican	1%	
Other Christian	3%	

Islam	18%
Hinduism	13%
Buddhism	6%
Chinese folk religions	4%
Shintoism	2%
Judaism	0.3%
Other religions	5%

Source: *Guinness Book of Answers*

Irrespective of the numbers of followers faiths have, it is when religions and religious groups come directly into our lives, either quite literally on the doorstep, such as Jehovah's Witnesses, or through the media, that we instinctively turn to our established church, the Church of England, to see what is its reaction.

A visit from a Jehovah's Witness might well make us brush up on the church's views on Armageddon. When the papers reported the death threat on Salman Rushdie we expected the Church of England to come to the defence of free speech.

It is when a culture clash of religions is underpinned by law that intolerance breaks out. Most Christians would rightly think that we should be intolerant of the Islamic law when a British subject is liable to become a victim of it in this country. The understandable view is that we don't agree with a lot of Islamic law, or the attitude that Muslim men have towards women, but as long as it doesn't affect us we won't interfere. Correspondingly, that goes with the view that when the faith of others impinges on Christian beliefs then we have a duty to take action.

It was in May 1999 that Britain, as a Christian country, took what Janet Daley called, 'a step towards defining the limits of multi-culturalism', when a High Court judge ordered an investigation to see if a 17-year-old Asian girl, a British subject, had been forced against her will to fly with her parents to India to enter into an arranged marriage with one of two men, neither of whom she had met. The girl, with her consent, was made a ward of court under the judicial protection of the British High Commission in India. The judge decided that the girl had been abducted and her parents were ordered to return her to the UK. This almost unnoticed example could well set a precedent for future religious/cultural clashes in our country. Our legal system, designed by politicians but based on historic Christian culture, is rooted in case law. Precedents are set for the future. As Janet Daley wrote (*Daily Telegraph*, 1 June 1999): 'It means that Britain has ruled that the freedom of ethnic minorities to maintain their own ethical priorities can be superseded, not only by the technicalities of law, but by the homegrown concepts of individual freedom and equality.' This will have far-reaching effects. Will British politicians allow the state to subsidize Muslim schools to offer an education that as a matter of principle gives less opportunities to girls than to boys, for instance?

This has come about when many parts of Christendom were moving towards some kind of rationale with other faiths. Then, on one of their own doorsteps, they are pulled up short.

At the same time, in parts of Asia, many Hindus have been attacking the Christian culture. In Gujarat, in India, churches have been burned to the ground, missionaries murdered and nuns stoned. There is evidence that some of the extreme Hindu nationalist Bharatiya Janata Party (BJP), which formed the government in 1998, at the very least condones these attacks – over 100 Christians have been attacked in one year, compared with under 50 from Independence to 1997.

Catholic and Protestant church leaders may well be moving towards a position of encouraging the recognition of God's spirit in all aspects of his creation, and therefore in other faiths, but on the ground it seems to be a slightly different story. Politicians have the same trouble. There is an exchange in Shakespeare's *Henry IV Part 1* that neatly sums up their predicament: Glendower says, 'I can call spirits from the vasty deep'. Hotspur replies, 'Why, so can I, or so can any man: but will they come when you do call for them?'

It is in the relationship between Christians and Jews that there is probably the greatest scope for working alliances. This is not only because of the common biblical base of Judaism and Christianity and all the historical connections – which now, as opposed to only a comparatively short time ago, help rather than hinder – it is also because the Jewish people have always played a strong role in public life in this country. The late Chief Rabbi Lord Jakobovits, unlike Cardinal Hume, accepted a life peerage and a seat in the House of Lords from Margaret Thatcher. She was so enthralled by his tales of how the Jews who settled in New York asked nothing from the state but formed self-supporting communities that she took his advice and read the Old Testament right through, taking great delight in asking her Cabinet ministers such questions as, 'Which is the only book in the Old Testament in which God is never mentioned?' (it's Esther). The Council of Christians and Jews has its own Parliamentary All-Party and Both Houses Interest Group Committee. The UK Council of Christians and Jews is one of the oldest bodies of its type in the world, dating from 1942. There are five Presidents: Dr Jonathan Sacks, the Chief Rabbi; the Greek Orthodox Archbishop of Great Britain; the Cardinal Archbishop of Westminster; the Archbishop of Canterbury; the Moderator of the Free Church Federal Council; and the Moderator of the General Assembly of the Church of Scotland. This is an organization that stretches out both vertically and horizontally to all the memberships of its various congregations, and at grass-roots level many congregations have mutually benefited by exchange visits. The Jewish communities have an excellent record in efficient and effective campaigning on issues of public concern and make great allies in any across-the-board lobbying exercise.

Another organization whose stance should always be considered and taken into consideration when campaigning is the World Council of Churches. This body, with headquarters in Geneva, Switzerland, was set up in 1948. Its aim is to promote unity among the many different Christian churches. The 324 member churches of the WCC have adherents in more than 100 countries. With the exception of Roman Catholicism, virtually all Christian traditions are included in the WCC's membership.

The policies of the Council are determined by the delegates of the member churches meeting in Assembly about every seven years, so there is ample time to organize any lobbying based either at them or from them. In its early days it did some outstanding work in presenting the problems of racism to the world, and it is able to get the ear of some government ministers in some parts of the world – that is where reliable research is needed!

In a multiracial, multifaith world, with ever-growing ease of communication and travel, for more and more people the role of 'mission' as understood at the start of the century has changed. Then it was a case of 'get as many as you can'. Denominations and some faiths poached off each other. But both the activity and the meaning of the word have changed. A missionary in 1900 would be baffled going into a social services meeting, or a university workshop, or a political focus group, to find that they were all working on 'mission statements'. Mission is now defining a desirable objective. In this country the spiritual leader of the established church, the Archbishop of Canterbury, has set out his mission for relationships with other faiths. Lambeth Palace says of the Archbishop, 'His preferred method of dialogue is that he should tell his story and listen to theirs as well'.

13

Disestablishment

IN *Alice's Adventures Through the Looking Glass*, Alice says to Humpty Dumpty, 'I don't know what you mean by "Glory".' Humpty Dumpty smiles contemptuously and replies, 'Of course, you don't – till I tell you. I mean a nice knock-down argument for you.'

'But,' objects Alice, 'glory doesn't mean "a nice knock-down argument".'

'When I use a word,' says Humpty Dumpty, 'it means just what I choose it to mean – neither more nor less.'

This was a problem the Archbishop of Canterbury's Commission on Church and State ran into in 1970. The chairman, Professor Owen Chadwick, decreed: 'For us "establishment" means the laws which apply to the Church of England and not to other churches.'

Unfortunately, fifteen years earlier, in *The Spectator* (23 September 1955), Henry Fairlee had given a different and wider definition:

> By the 'Establishment' I do not mean only the centres of official power – though they are certainly part of it – but rather the whole matrix of official and social relations within which power is exercised. The exercise of power in Britain (more specifically in England) cannot be understood unless it is recognised that it is exercised socially. Anyone who has at any point been close to the exercise of power will know what I mean when I say that the 'Establishment' can be seen at work in the activities of, not only the Prime Minister, the Archbishop of Canterbury and the Earl Marshall, but of such lesser mortals as the chairman of the Arts Council, the Director-General of the BBC, and even the Editor of the *Times Literary Supplement*, not to mention divinities like Lady Violet Bonham-Carter.

This was an article that caught the imagination of the time. Newspapers, magazines and radio seized on this view of England. Sir Robert Boothby MP said:

It was never confined, as is commonly supposed, to what used to be known as the 'Upper Ten'. Nor did it embrace all the Cabinet ministers of the day. It always included the reigning Archbishop of Canterbury, Editor of *The Times*, Governor of the Bank of England and Secretary to the Cabinet.

Peter Cook, John Wells, John Bird, John Fortune and Jonathan Miller set up a satirical nightclub in Soho and called it the 'Establishment'. Members of the establishment loved it. Professor David Marquand, a former Labour MP, gave Jeremy Paxman a quote for his book, *Friends in High Places*: 'While governments came and went [some] institutions seemed to go on for ever: the civil service, the universities, the Church of England, the BBC.'

Note how in all three quotes either the Archbishop of Canterbury or the Church of England figures prominently as part of the 'Establishment'. No matter what the Archbishop's Commission might hope, there was never a chance that their report and discussion on it could be confined to a narrow legal definition of establishment. 'Establishment' as well as being shorthand for national authority was also an attitude of mind which as far as some people were concerned stifled freedom and discouraged enterprise and new thinking. This was expressed in the Church of England by many young clergy who felt that the church being so closely involved in the national authority of the state was shackling their attempts to bring the word of Christ to the people. A feeling for disestablishing, if not a campaign, was reemerging.

The first modern thoughts on disestablishment were expressed by John Keble in a sermon at Oxford on 14 July 1833. Parliament had reduced the number of bishops in the minority Church of Ireland, a measure which was agreed on all sides (apart from one or two of the Irish bishops being removed) to be a sensible and sound act. It was a catalyst for Keble to question whether Parliament should have control over church organization.

Eleven years later in 1844 the Society for the Liberation of Religion from State Patronage and Control was founded. Another organization, the Church Defence Institution, which was set up in 1860, became the Church Committee for Church Defence and Church Instruction in 1896. In Victorian times it was a subject which both politicians and clergy took extremely seriously. Pressure for disestablishment came from many churchmen but was opposed by most politicians. Two Bills for Disestablishment were proposed in the eighteenth century. One in 1871 was lost by 374 votes to 89 and one a year later by 295 to 61. At that time senior members of the Church of England expressed themselves willing for disestablishment; but there was a sticking point. Disestablishment led to disendowment; the bishops were unwilling to lose their cathedrals.

The debate over establishment was of tremendous interest to those active in public life in the nineteenth century and a debate raged and decision were made affecting the organization of religious life in the British Isles comparable with the decisions made at the end of the twentieth century on the organization of political life in the British Isles. But we did not have such an informed debate!

Scotland had its own established church long before its parliament was returned. The established Church of Scotland is reformed and evangelical in doctrine and presbyterian in constitution. In 1560 the jurisdiction of the Roman Catholic Church in Scotland was abolished and the first assembly of the Church of Scotland ratified the Confession of Faith drawn up by a committee including John Knox. In 1592 Parliament passed an Act guaranteeing the liberties of the church and its presbyterian government. After the Civil War the church was placed under the bishops for a short time but in 1689 it reverted to its presbyterian organization – confirmed by statute in 1707. In a dispute over state interference the Free Church of Scotland was formed in 1843. After state patronage was abolished in Scotland most of the clergy joined with the United Presbyterian Church, forming the united Free Church of Scotland.

The governing body is the General Assembly, presided over by a moderator chosen from among its own members; in contrast to the Archbishop of Canterbury who is appointed by the Prime Minister. This is a key point made by those who favour the disestablishment of the Church of England. (At the Annual Assembly the Monarch is represented – or is occasionally there in person – by a Lord High Commissioner who is appointed by the Crown and attends as an observer.)

The Church of Wales was finally disestablished in 1920. Throughout the nineteenth century there had been an estrangement of the majority of the Welsh people from Anglicanism. The completion of the movement was delayed by discussion about the extent of disendowment and then by the First World War. Eventually it was decided that the church would lose all artifacts dating before 1662 but would keep all cathedrals and churches. Incumbents were protected and the state gave the Church in Wales a final pay-off of 1 million pounds. The Church in Wales consists of around 100,000 members in six sees. There are 1142 parishes and about 700 stipendiary clergy.

There is a governing body comprising the six bishops and elected members of clergy and laity. This body elects the Archbishop of Wales from one of the six bishops; again, a point made with force by those who propose disestablishment for the Church of England. However, the Westminster Parliament did not let the Church in Wales go easily. Before the 1920 Act, bills had been presented to Parliament to disestablish in 1886, 1892, 1894, 1909 and 1912, and all defeated.

The Anglican Church in Ireland had never secured the allegiance of the people in a Roman Catholic country, and in 1871 the Irish Church was disestablished and disendowed. There are around 350,000 Anglicans in the island of Ireland. The Church in Ireland divides under the organization of two Archbishops, one in Dublin and one in Armagh. There are ten bishops. (In Eire there are five Roman Catholic Archbishops and 22 bishops.)

Disestablishment was very much in vogue in Europe at that time. The Church of France disestablished in 1906.

The Victorian debate in England was vigorous. A Fellow of Balliol, W. G. Ward, argued that greater freedom would lead to greater integrity as the church would not only be able to order its own liturgy but it could escape from the deferential attitude it was forced to adopt towards the civil authorities. In 1844 he wrote:

> No single bishop can so much as appoint the Ember Day Prayer to be used on the week preceding his day for ordinations, should he see cause to change the latter. The only alterations, now ever made in our Prayer Book, are made by an Order of the Queen in Council.

The views expressed over a hundred years ago are still resolutely held by others, such as Peter Cornwell, a former Church of England Priest, now a Roman Catholic. Here is John Keble, quoted in Peter Cornwell's book, *Church and Nation*:

> We are the one religious body in the Queen's dominions to which the following privileges are expressly denied: To declare our own doctrines, to confirm, vary and repeal our own Canons, to have a say in the nomination of our own chief pastors, to grant or withold our own sacraments according to our own proper rules. If these disadvantages are inseparable from the position of our establishment then establishment must go.

Some of that position have modified their views, but here are Peter Cornwell's own words later in his book:

> In looking for an open church which has integrity, I find establishment tripping us into the pit of phoney openness ... What should the Church

do? Prophesy and engage in the political task. What should the Church be? An open church united in the affirmation of one faith. It is only for the sake of renewal of the church in holy catholicity, in apostolic service and in unity that disestablishment makes sense.

The argument for disestablishment is not just to achieve a national church of integrity, it is also to make the church more effective in its out-reaching tasks of prophecy and political engagement. Those arguing in favour of disestablishment make the point that there is today, and has been for some time, a clear split between those who go to church in England and those who don't. At the time of the Reformation, it is claimed, everybody believed in God and religion was a daily part of the life of all. The nation state was a holy state. Life was not compartmentalized into temporal and spiritual and God watched over everything. It then made sense to have a national church because it reflected, indeed was inseparable from, the life of the nation.

But that has changed. Statistics are used in many ways to show that church attendance is increasing or decreasing in some areas for some perceived reasons. Figures are also used to show that while church attendance is low, there is a large hinterland of people who regard themselves as members of the Church of England, even if they never go – like Manchester United having the most enormous supporters club, 80 per cent of whom will rarely go to a match. One reason for disestablishment is that a club of which everybody is automatically a member, without either paying anything or doing anything, can't be a club of any real value.

The argument is also made that the Church of England is no longer the only club around. This tends to come not so much from those inside the established church but from those outside who see at least the higher levels of the Church of England enjoying an unfair advantage in the social and political battles of life. This argument is often extended to include the House of Lords. In a newly reformed second chamber why have only Anglican bishops as of right? Why not Roman Catholics, Methodists, Baptists and members of other faiths? Why not have them in their own right and not dependent on the patronage of a life peerage. The trouble with good intentions like this is that sometimes the supposed beneficiaries are not as grateful as the reformers expect. Some churches would not wish to be identified with the governing classes, feeling it might detract from their biblical bias to the poor.

Indeed one of the strongest arguments of disestablishers is that the

Church of England's association with the trappings and symbols of power and government – though not perhaps the actuality – is a major difficulty in carrying out their role as the body of Christ. This argument might be taken a good deal more seriously by those outside the church if they didn't see the Church of England itself following the typical social structure of giving more responsibility, access to influence, power, money, trappings and privileges to those in least daily contact with the poor, the weak and the hungry.

The case for disestablishment can be made at two levels: the general and the particular. The general case rests on the grounds that a church so closely tied to the organization of the state is not now appropriate; it ties in members of the church, both clergy and laity, with the governing class. These are not the right cultural or social mores for the church to be effective in doing Christ's work on earth. For the sake of its own integrity the church must be free to make its own decisions.

The particular case rests on two factors. It is wrong that the church should not be ultimately responsible for its own liturgy and forms of worship. It is wrong that the leaders of the Church of England are appointed by the Crown on the advice of the Prime Minister of the day, who may not even be a practising Christian.

There is a third argument which straddles the general and the particular. If a nation has its own established church it can use it on specific occasions to endow specific acts of government with spurious and official Christian authority.

Attitudes toward disestablishment ebb and flow like the tides. At times during the last century it seemed more likely than not to happen. There was a general relaxed feeling after the Second World War that disestablishment was on its way – something like votes for women; there might be a nudge needed here or there, but it would probably come in due course. Then two things happened. The Church of England, having conferred with Parliament and the Government and been told that only if they disestablished would they have complete freedom to appoint their own bishops, backed down. Second, the fuss over the introduction of the Alternative Service Book, and the perceived abandonment of the Book of Common Prayer, brought forth an army of nominal Christians (if only the church had devised a strategy to keep them) and awoke some Members of Parliament to the fact that they and not the bishops or the General Synod were actually responsible for the church of the nation. These two factors enabled the establishment, in every sense of the term, to dig in.

There may now be a turn of the tide. One of the most astute observers of religious matters in this country, Clifford Longley, discovered that in November 1998 a meeting had been held at the highest level of the mainstream ecumenical body in England, CTE (Churches Together in England), under the chairmanship of the Bishop of Winchester, to discuss the established status of the Church of England. Longley wrote in the *Daily Telegraph* (15 January 1999):

> It (the meeting) took place at the end of November though news has only just leaked out, which suggests how touchy the matter is assumed to be. Indeed, some officials inside the Church of England would be very unhappy to be praised for being bold and courageous, as they are keen to play down the consultation. It is, they say, simply an opportunity to explain. To them – and they seem to include Lambeth Palace – the church–state link is non-negotiable.
>
> This is technically correct, though not as a result of any wish on the Church's part. The Church of England is not established because it chose to be: it is established by laws made by Parliament ... Talk of disestablishment will not go away ... It has moved up the agenda and is still rising.

As with most discussions in public life there are masses of hidden agendas. It would be difficult for the Church of England to move closer to the Methodist Church – other than at parish level where in some cases there are significant overlapping congregations – while Parliament has the final say in its affairs.

The Venerable George Austin, former Archdeacon of York, has yet another agenda. In a letter to the papers he says:

> The Prince of Wales is surely right to wish to be a defender of all the faiths in the multi-faith and multicultural nation over which he will one day reign. It is proper that consideration should be given at this stage to the form and content of a coronation ceremony in the light of that diversity, not present in any comparable degree in 1953 ... Is this not the opportunity for the church to abandon the status given by establishment ... Is it a vain hope that with the first coronation of the new Millennium we might return to being the unprivileged servant Church of the New Testament?

Some who favour disestablishing are looking to the events in Sweden to see if that might be a role model. In 1995 the Swedish Parliament accepted a proposal from the General Synod of the Church of Sweden that there should be a recognition in law that society and membership of the established church were not necessarily the same. The Roman Catholic Church has grown in the country and there has been immigration from Latin America, Southern Europe and the Middle East. Over the last twenty years a Muslim community of some 200,000 has developed. Under the proposals for separation, regulations have been drawn up defining membership and giving the church legal authority over its own laws. There is also a 'Church Fee' established for all who join the church, means-tested, based on the finances of individual members, which includes the cost of a funeral. Matters of heritage and historic record have been decided and the disestablished church comes into being in the year 2000.

In the past, supporters of disestablishment have missed the tide each time it seemed to be running their way. There were reasons for this. One was that most of them were already working in an extremely active way inside the Church of England and hadn't either the time to take on board what they would need to do in campaigning terms, or the time and effort to do it. To succeed in such a campaign it is useless to believe that a vague feeling that the time is right for disestablishment will grow into a ground-swell of opinion leading to an Act of Parliament by popular acclaim. It has to be worked at. Those who feel strongly about change, who really believe that Christ's work can be done better by disestablishing, have a duty to their beliefs to become involved in effective planning.

At the moment disestablishment will only come about by one of five ways: stealth; unilateral declaration of independence; schism; agreed legislation; contested legislation. Stealth could be a very effective operational way to run a campaign: to so remove all the symbols and trappings of establishment that even if in name the church was still established it was not in practice. It could even be that the time is right for this approach. The Prince of Wales is encouraged to become 'Defender of all the Faiths'. Thus leaders of other faiths cluster round at the coronation, and while the new King might keep the title of Supreme Governor it would be nominal. The church would then embrace enthusiastically the recommendations of the Home Affairs Select Committee of the House of Commons, quoted here:

Note 125: The second issue drawn to our attention, the eligibility of Christian ministers of religion, is not one of major importance, either in terms of the principle involved or in practical terms. It is nevertheless a good example of the way in which British electoral laws have developed in a piecemeal fashion and are in need of bringing up to date.

Note 126: Professor Blackburn has pointed out that finding the answer to the question, 'Can a priest stand for Parliament?' involves reference to nine separate acts, dating back to the 16th century. The results show a picture almost totally lacking in consistency or, in modern terms, any rational basis. Restrictions apply only to Christian ministers, and not to those of any faith. They differ between Anglican priests, Roman Catholic priests, and non-conformist clergy. And the position differs in England, Scotland and Wales. Furthermore, some such ministers who are otherwise barred from being MPs can resign their ministry in order to serve while others cannot.

Note 127: These restrictions seem to us to be out of place in modern times. There should be no restriction on ministers of religion becoming Members of Parliament, and certainly no distinction between those of different faiths or of different Christian traditions. Whether such persons should serve as an elected representative should be a matter for the rules and customs of their own faiths or churches and for the electorate, and need not be restricted by law. We therefore recommend that, with one exception, all restrictions on ministers of religion standing for, and serving as, Members of Parliament be removed: the exception would be in respect of all serving bishops of the Church of England who, for so long as places are reserved for the senior bishops in the House of Lords, should remain ineligible to serve as Members of the Commons. (*Hansard* 10 September 1998; Order 127)

If this was enacted by Parliament, which is an extension of what the General Synod proposed in 1982, then the clergy would have strong grounds for saying that Parliament has now agreed that the clergy no longer form the Fourth Estate of the Realm, and has thus itself removed a large section of 'Establishment'.

Unfortunately this recommendation has been greeted with no response at all from the clergy. Not, I think, through any lack of real interest, but because no one has told them. Yet the implications, apart from chipping away at 'Establishment', are fascinating. An elected member of the clergy could openly attack the government of the day on the floor of the House of Commons – a practical way of chipping away at the Establishment. Clergy could discuss amongst themselves whether they wanted to be selected as candidates in existing parties or form their own Clerical Party, as happens in some countries. The General Synod could even decide if it wanted to put up official 'Church of England' candidates – a sure way to encourage the movement towards disestablishment.

Moving by stealth could also entail not bothering to bring notices about changes in worship to Parliament, but just to encourage priests to have greater flexibility in interpreting the liturgy. At all levels priests would follow the lead of their 'Defender' and encourage ministers of other denominations and faiths to do duty on national and local civic occasions. The bishops would gradually withdraw from the House of Lords. By stealth, over a period of time, the Church of England would simply not be carrying out its duties as the nation's church.

In the current climate of opinion, and given the personnel involved, the second way by which disestablishment might come about is unlikely. Those in favour of disestablishment persuade by argument and elegance the rest of the church unilaterally to renounce the establishment and give up all their endowments.

The more likely way than that would be the third way, for a group inside the Church of England to feel so strongly about the matter that they are able to gather a large enough body around them to break away from the main Church of England, leaving in place a rump that is simply too small to carry out the duties of an established church.

The most likely way that disestablishment would come about is by legislation, either agreed or opposed. In both cases very similar operations would have to be carried out. Either the politicians would have to be convinced by the correctness of the case beforehand in a series of private meetings, or they would have to be persuaded in public on the floor of both Houses at Westminster and in the committee corridors. In planning any campaign those who are in favour of disestablishment have to take on board not just what they see as the 'rightness' of their cause but also the practicalities of convincing the politicians. They sometimes seem not to understand that it is absolutely and entirely in the hands of Westminster politicians as to whether or not this country has an established church. Whatever the wishes of the Church of England the decision will be made by Parliament; not necessarily the government of the day because there might well be a free vote, with parties not applying the whip. This is something else those campaigning must take into account in their plans for lobbying. One thing is certain: without effective lobbying it won't happen.

14

Establishment

COLIN Buchanan, Bishop of Woolwich, has written one of the most definitive and much-admired books about disestablishment, *Cut the Connection: Disestablishment and the Church of England* (1994). But I wonder if his supporters in the pews understand the massive amount of time and energy, not to mention skill and perhaps cunning, that will be needed to wrest the Church of England from the power of the establishment. It has to be done by Parliament. In the most blatant analysis it is like the Hong Kong situation: the wishes of the people matter not; it is in the gift of the politicians.

This means that in the best possible scenario the Church of England will have managed to gain enough support among its own member-ship that the General Synod votes by a massive majority to ask the Archbishop to set in hand talks with the Government to bring forward a Disestablishment Bill. Already there are three problems. First, the lobby inside the church has to find the time and expertise to convince the man and woman in the pew and then the synods at various levels that this is the right way forward. Second, there has to be a massive, clear and unfudged vote in favour; if not, the Ecclesiastical Committee of both Houses, the Privy Council, the Home Office, the Department of Culture and the Prime Minister, in turn, will simply explain that without an overwhelming majority there is no way the bill can become a government measure; and as a private measure it would not get either parliamentary time or support. Third, the Archbishop must be completely committed, otherwise there is no way he (or she – thinking of the future) can begin to sell the idea to the Prime Minister.

If it does get that far the opposition will be formidable. To start with, a disestablished church cannot have the Head of State as its leader – by whatever name she or he is called. That would call into question the whole role of the Monarch and it could well be that the establishment, in Henry Fairlee's terms, close ranks around the sovereign, including the Prime Minister and enough members of both Houses to block all progress on the bill. This would be an area of such delicate diplomacy between Buckingham Palace, Lambeth Palace, Church House, 10 Downing Street and both Houses of Parliament that I suspect those inside the church pressing for change would just not have the experience to deal with it. The Queen, as is well known, takes her coronation vows with extreme seriousness and devotion.

If the debate inside Parliament does start, then undoubtedly the first rule of lobbying, which I referred to in an earlier chapter, will come into effect. An opposition group will develop in favour of keeping the establishment. This body will have the tremendous advantage of time. The passage of the bill through the various committees and chambers, with all the highways and by-ways that have to be explored – the future of historic records, artifacts, the seats of bishops in the House of Lords, the employment status of clergy, the future cost of church schools, the position of army chaplains, the ownership of the Royal Peculiars, such as Westminster Abbey, etc., and the media attention this will attract – will give those opposed the chance to organize.

Thousands of letters will pour in from those described by G. Davie (*Religion in Britain since 1945*) as 'believing without belonging', asking their MPs to stop the vandals destroying their church. Look what happened on a much, much smaller scale in 1999 when the relationship between bishops and parish church wardens came up for discussion. Following a dispute in the Norwich diocese where five Norfolk parishes declared themselves independent in protest at the dismissal of their vicar, the General Synod proposed new legislation to enable a bishop to suspend any church warden for 'good or reasonable cause'. The General Synod Legislative Committee took this proposal to the All-Party (both Houses) Ecclesiastical Committee at Westminster to ask them to bring the necessary legislation forward in the House of Commons. The Committee refused and the church just hadn't seen it coming. The Synod tried to reassure the politicians that the bill was about protecting worshippers from child-abusers and those likely to bring their church into disrepute. John Gummer, a former Cabinet minister and former member of the General Synod (he became a Roman Catholic over the question of the ordination of women) said: 'The Church of England has not needed provision to suspend church wardens for 700 years and it does not need it now. They have come up with a solution for a problem that does not exist.'

The Archbishop of York, Dr David Hope, Chairman of the Legislative Committee of the General Synod, countered with the opinion that it was the duty of church wardens to serve as officers to the bishop as well as represent the laity and the parish. He added: 'There have been rare occurrences in the past and are likely to be in the future where the parish experiences a serious problem where we need some means of suspending a church warden.' The lack of preparation in putting forward their case was underlined by the fact that, before the meeting, the Church of England had not even persuaded the Church Commissioner who deals with questions on the Church of England in the House of Commons, Stuart Bell MP, of the correctness of their case. Bell said:

> This had no chance. I am amazed they even tried to put it forward. There has to be machinery to suspend a church warden convicted of a crime, for instance. But the idea that they could be suspended because it 'seemed right' to the bishop is the language of the abuse of power. I have had hundreds of letters from people from all over the country in protest at this.

That was a telling point. On what was a measure which would seem of little interest to most of the population those who were opposed got organized. They identified the most relevant MPs to write to and targeted them. A lot of the letters came from the 25,000 lay church wardens, many of whom feel that they are as much 'the church' as bishops. If internal opposition in the Church of England can link up successfully with Members of Parliament to block a measure which went ahead with the full support of the General Synod, it suggests that the General Synod needs to get closer in touch with its members and also develop a greater political sense. Those with political sense should have seen there were two fatal flaws in what they were trying to do. There were no criteria given for what constituted 'reasonable' cause. What one bishop might find acceptable behaviour in a church warden another might not tolerate; it was giving the bishops 'unreasonable' power. Second, there was no balance of accountable democracy. If a bishop had that power and exercised it, to whom was he accountable for his actions? The Westminster system of democracy, flawed as it is, does at least have a tradition of trying to build into institutions a moderating influence of checks and balances. Here there were none.

This was a small thing. But if the Church of England can mishandle this in such a spectacular fashion the mind boggles at the kind of opposition it could stir up – from a much wider hinterland – in any proposal it brought forward for the church to become disestablished.

Another point that the supporters of disestablishment may not have realized is that like all campaigns they will be joined by allies they may not particularly want. And the 'establishment' will ruthlessly use that fact by exploiting the views of those getting on the bandwagon as the substantive views of the main campaign. I am thinking especially here of those non-believers who hold that it is quite wrong for there to be any close link between church and state and are working in a humanist way for a much more secular country. They will jump at a chance to drive a wedge between the church and the state. They will, in effect, be saying, 'Yes it is high time we agreed that it is wrong for the Christians to be so close to the decision-making process in what is now a secular country.' This in turn will lead the supporters of establishment to say to the disestablishers, 'Look what you have done. You are now publicly encouraging the view that we are not a Christian country. What kind of message is that sending out to people?'

The other group of people who will support the campaign for disestablishment are those who don't necessarily object to there being a link between religions and the Government but do object to that link being monopolised by the Church of England. As they see no way of their denomination, faith or cult ever receiving the same treatment they are happy for what they see as the undue influence of the Church of England being reduced to their own level. This again gives the establishment ammunition. They say to those working for disestablishment, 'Look, at the moment, however unsatisfactory it might be, the church does have access to the Government. Take that away and it means the authorities of the nation are subject to no exposure to official religion at all.'

I have dwelt on the difficulties those campaigning for disestablishment face in a chapter headed 'Establishment' quite deliberately. It is the best way of showing the strength of the 'establishment'; it is a way of defining what is more than part of the unwritten constitution but is a whole national concept. By examining how difficult it is to attack, its very nature can be seen.

But, why are supporters of the established church so keen to maintain the status quo? What are the benefits they see, which to supporters of disestablishment are disadvantages? It must be said that some of the benefits can be seen in a slightly dubious light in terms of personal vanity and status. Many people will enjoy the perceived privileges of belonging to a religious organization where their leader, the Archbishop of Canterbury, is ranked immediately after members of the Royal Family as the highest in the land. The real question is – are there actual advantages and does the Church of England use them effectively in the work of Christ?

The first advantage that the supporters of establishment put forward is that there is an historic link between church and state which goes back well before the Reformation and is part of the fabric of our society. Interwoven in that fabric is the observable fact that people use the Church of England for marriages, baptisms, and funerals in a way that they don't feel they can ask to use Roman Catholic or Methodist churches. One vicar said this to me:

> I often get called out to talk to families where a death has occurred, even though the family concerned has never come to church. They call me out because they live in my parish and as one of them said, I don't go to church, but I 'feel' I am a member of the Church of England. They don't 'feel' so free to call out a priest or minister from another denomination – let alone someone from another faith.

This is a duty which clergy in the Church of England have and is recognized by the public at large. I am not saying that ministers from other denominations wouldn't respond in a loving and sensitive way if approached; but, on the whole, they are not approached. This is a similar duty to that of a Member of Parliament: there is responsibility to all in their patch, irrespective of views.

Being a national church means that no matter how stretched, the Church of England has clergy covering every square mile of the country. All of us in England live in a parish of the Church of England. The actual name 'parish' is often used by people to describe where they live, especially in rural areas, and the very name for local councils – Parish Councils – is yet another example of how historically church and state are as closely interwoven at the (lowest) level of local government as they are at the (highest) level of national government in the Palace of Westminster.

Given that position, argue the supporters of establishment, why risk changing it? Once the jigsaw is broken it won't be possible to put it back together if the new arrangements don't work. Their argument runs that it may be inconvenient that we have to go to Parliament to have changes in our forms of worship approved, but that only happens a few times each century. Balanced against that is an inherited structure which enables Christianity to impinge on people's lives where it otherwise might not. Who can either quantify or qualify those moments in peoples lives? The argument continues: are we going to risk throwing all that away, and possibly end up as a self-regarding cult, making it more difficult to interact with others?

There is a real problem with definition. What is the Church of England? Is it its buildings? If the church and state break links, to whom do the buildings belong? In the arguments about endowment in Wales and Ireland there were strong views expressed that the actual churches and cathedrals belonged to the people for all time, not the current clergy of that time. If the Church of England stops being the established church then it has to be defined by its membership. Membership will not be everybody in the parish as it is at the moment, many of whom exercise the right to be married in their parish church. Will it be those on the electoral register? Will they have to pay a fee, as in Sweden? Will the church be allowed to make its own rules like other voluntary associations? No longer having the patronage of the state, will it still be able to escape the requirements on the laws of equal opportunity?

The fundamental point behind questions like these is, will all these actions bring the church closer or make it more remote from the lives of ordinary people? Those in favour of disestablishment say that a more focused church, in charge of its own affairs, unencumbered with the position of the Archbishop of Canterbury as an automatic member of the great and the good, not having to bother about bishops wasting time in the House of Lords, will be a church of greater effect. It will be a church of greater integrity and therefore have a greater impact in doing the work of Christ. The very bottom line of the argument to stay established is that disestablishment is too great a gamble.

That is a strong bottom line from which to fight – especially in alliance with the rallying cry of 'Whose Church?' Is the Church of England a slightly mystical body belonging in some way to both God and the people, or is it a clearly defined body belonging to those people who at any one time happen to be its leaders, stewards and members? The attitude of many politicians if faced with a demand for disestablishment is to argue that the Church of England belongs neither to the Archbishops, bishops, General Synod, clergy and committed laity – at any particular time – to claim as their own; nor does it belong to the politicians in Parliament – at any particular time – to give from the people to a specific interest group. I believe that this is a genuine attitude on behalf of most MPs. They are safeguarding the interests of their electorate. But, it must also be taken into account that there would be few popular votes in favour of disestablishment, which is why those supporters do not press for a referendum on the matter. Every MP I have talked with has said that even if the people in the pews followed the lead of the bishops and the General Synod, assuming that point was ever reached, and became actively committed to a campaign for disestablishment, the next circle of the hinterland – the 'Christians' who (a) rarely and (b) never went to church – would oppose the measure. Not only that, they would be activated by committed Christians who were against disestablishment to write to, and to see, their MPs; sign petitions; lobby the bishops; send letters to the newspapers and speak on local radio. Public figures would emerge to support establishment (and 'the establishment') at least as able to gain media attention as those leading the disestablishment cause. It would draw into this public debate, probably against the wishes of those in the church arguing for disestablishment, those wanting the measure to advance the cause of a secular society. There would be a real danger that the debate would not be about whether or not to have an established church but whether we should move to be an even more secular nation. At this point I would anticipate that the might of Henry Fairlee's 'Establishment' would move in and the subject would be removed from the national agenda. Or rather, it would stay on the agenda like one of those items perpetually classed under 'Any Other Business'.

If the Church of England is to remain established surely there are positive advantages that can be used in the service of Christ. The church by its very nature is a campaigning organization, in two ways. First, it has a duty of mission to spread the word of God in whatever way it considers most appropriate. Second, it is the body of Christ on earth, to do the practical things which Christians believe are important. Compared with all other campaigning organizations the church has tremendous advantages. It has the things which other charities and lobbying groups value and work to obtain: a brand name which is instinctively recognized; royal patronage; access to opinion-formers, decision-makers and government; a professional staff at Church House and Lambeth Palace – many of whom come from the ranks of the civil service, who understand the business of government; a network of local organizations and an army of volunteers willing to do the drudgery work. Thanks to the fact that it is an established church, it has a leader, the Archbishop of Canterbury, who can be effective on the world stage, in a way that is out of proportion to the actual numbers in the church. It also has a professional level of dedicated staff and a well-regarded training programme.

Of course, the Church is different. Its campaigning programme and similar activities are only part of its function. Many would argue not even the most important part of its function. But it is a part, and a highly visible and observed part at international, national and local level. Compared with any other campaigning group the Church of England has the best-structured access to government both formally and informally. Yet, I wonder how often on a regular basis a bishop with a seat in the House of Lords sits down with some of the members of his diocese and says, in effect: 'Look. I've got official and unofficial access to both information and people in government. How can I best use it this month in the service of Christ?'

The theological basis for this was spelt out by the Rev. Pete Broadbent, Archdeacon of Northolt, in an essay, 'The Political Imperative' in Gavin Reid's book *Hope for the Church of England*:

> The words of the risen Jesus to his disciples: 'Peace be with you. As the Father sent me, so I send you' (John 20:21). We as disciples of the Jesus who was sent with good news in word and deed, walk in the shoes of our master. (For that is what discipleship means.) We are sent to the world as he was. Evangelism and social action, the twin prongs of mission, are our calling ... God incarnate points us away from the unhappy dualism of body and spirit that has perverted Christian theology for too long and reminds us that the Hebrew concept of the person as unity is the biblical idea upon which Christian theology is based. So, a Christian taking the incarnation seriously will take the life of this world seriously, for it was on this stage that the word became flesh.

Later Broadbent quotes the speeches of Bishop Bell, and refers to the British Nationality Act, the Urban Priority Areas, and concern with the nuclear bomb, as reasons and examples showing that 'The church cannot keep out of politics without neglecting its true role'. Broadbent, who was one of the most effective university chaplains of his generation, also draws a comparison between working – in 'established' worlds – as a priest and as a politician:

> A useful parallel is that of the elected councillor or MP who, though only elected by those supporting his or her party has to represent and deal with the problems of the whole of his or her constituency. There is a distinction to be drawn here between the abuse of one's God-given role as teacher and pastor by using the pulpit for political purposes (illegitimate) and the capacity of the minister to exercise a political role in the community as part of his or her overall ministry.

Edward Carpenter, Archdeacon of Westminster Abbey, wrote in 1966, in *The English Church: Church and State in History*:

An established church cannot even be tempted to regard the Christian ethic as relevant only to man's personal life while leaving his civic and national responsibilities untouched. It cannot – if it is true to itself – affect, for a moment, to despise politics, to see them as essentially a somewhat dirty business; must hold a high view of them. An established church recognises that to serve society governmentally is for some Christians a vocational constraint: and that matters of law within and between States are finally subject to the divine will and need to be lifted into the world of grace. This means that an established Church has at times the responsibility of sitting in judgment and all the time of challenging the State with the claims of God's Kingdom, though it will do this as deeply involved and in no holier than thou spirit.

Inside the Church of England, questioning the position of the established church has nearly always come from some of the leaders of both clergy and laity at various levels. There has never been a grass-roots ground-swell clamour for disestablishment. In part this is a tribute to the traditional ability of the English establishment to absorb (and take a bit of notice of) desires for change. The established church has a duty to use its advantages in the work of Christ.

15

The Millennium Factor

ONE factor common to both politicians and priests is a desire to reflect on the nature of life and perhaps try to identify some turning-point, which either has made a significant difference or is a point from which one sets off to a hopeful future. There are books full of such observations and yearnings:

> What then of ambition, that driving force that has been with me through boyhood, youth, doubt, manhood? What colour is ambition, does it ripen with time, or does it canker? What is one ambitious for, is it only oneself, or can one also be ambitious for our country? Who can separate the two, who can weigh them in the balance? All I know is that with my eyes open I have chosen the least trodden path. (David Owen, *Time to Declare*)

> For serious and lively debate to arise on this topic (establishment) would be no bad way of celebrating the hundred and fiftieth anniversary of Keble's Assize Sermon. (Peter Cornwell, *Church and Nation*)

> I sat down with the cheers of my colleagues, wets and dries, allies and opponents, Stalwarts and fainthearts, ringing in my ears, and began to think about what I would do next. (Margaret Thatcher, *The Downing Street Years*)

> We are still only at the beginning of our task. But the beginning is to try and be honest and to go on from there. (John Robinson, *Honest to God*)

> The world of politics will become increasingly complex over the coming years. The need to relate Christian faith to that world will become more and more crucial. The Church of England has a unique role in this regard. Whatever the government of the day or media critics of the church might wish to argue, the political imperative cannot be ducked. Rather we should hear the call of God's Kingdom and respond gladly,

knowing that in the end that Kingdom is the only enduring political structure. (Pete Broadbent, in Gavin Reid, *Hope for the Church of England*)

The advent of the millennium is an obvious turning-point for reflection and resolution for the future (New Year's resolutions multiplied by a factor of a thousand!). It is a natural meeting point of the spiritual and temporal world. The millennium is only being celebrated because Christianity has kept alive the hope and salvation offered by the birth, death and resurrection of Jesus Christ. It is being celebrated by a largely, if not secular at least non-Christian, world. Yet, in our own Christian country, with an established church, there has been prolonged discussion, first with the Conservative Government and then with New Labour, as to the part Christianity should play in the nation's most obvious manifestation of the millennium, the Dome at Greenwich. It was as though the politicians were pushing the priests aside and keeping them away from the agenda. New Labour had already given the impression that it wanted to exercise a high degree of control in politics. This was shown in its attitude to devolution, the question of London's elected mayor and its desire to keep its MPs 'on message'. It was even accused by members of its own party of having a 'control freak' tendency. Outside politics New Labour did this with a lighter touch and it may be that if the Conservatives had won the general election they too would have behaved in the same way.

Perhaps the politicians were influenced by the results of a poll published in the *Sunday Times* (7 February 1999) asking people who they thought provided the best moral and spiritual leadership in Britain today. They were given a choice of 35 figures to choose from. The result was: 1, Tony Blair; 2, the Archbishop of Canterbury; 3, Cardinal Basil Hume; 4, the Queen; 5, the Chief Rabbi.

The *Sunday Times* commented that Tony Blair 'once described the Labour Party as the party of Christianity and some observers see an evangelical style in his public appearances'. Professor of Sociology at Warwick University, James Beckford observed: 'Although church attendance is declining, many people have not lost their interest in religious and spiritual themes. Many of the statements Blair makes resonate with those who have not lost their spiritual musicality.' Christians should note with joy and hope that the Archbishop of Canterbury is at number 2 and Cardinal Hume at number 3. As one academic, Dr John Charmley, Reader in History at the University of East Anglia, said: 'With the Archbishop of Canterbury at number two overall it suggests we are not quite the nation of agnostics and atheists we purport to be.'

The coming of the millennium has given evidence that we are just as concerned with the big questions of why we are born if we are only going to die, and what happens when we do die, as we have ever been. It has certainly been the touchstone for numerous newspaper articles. Here is what Bryan Appleyard wrote in the *Sunday Times* under the heading, 'No Time Like The Present'. He is describing life, using the traditional image of life as a journey:

> Perhaps you can console yourself that, in travelling, you did your duty. But duty to what? Even if the future is better it will only be better relative to you. Future travellers will feel that their present is as inconclusive, as unsatisfactory as yours. No matter how much better their technology, they will be just as discontentedly dreaming of a better future that will never arrive. This journey into the future offers no meaning, no purpose, no peace, only movement. That is the dilemma in which, at the end of the second millennium of the Christian era, we find ourselves. We must go on, but we don't know why.

Tom Utley, writing in the *Daily Telegraph*, asks a more specific question under the heading 'Are we on the verge of a religious revival?' Like other writers, including Bryan Appleyard, he ties his thoughts to the millennium and writes:

> It was to be expected that the end of the second millennium of the Christian era would prompt a revival of religious feeling in the developed world ... Throughout my lifetime the march of science has been so astonishingly swift and exciting ... how implausible beside that is the story that God sent his Son down to earth to be born of a virgin in a stable, and crucified to redeem our sins. But, hang on says a voice inside most of us. There are some questions that scientists can never answer. All right, it may be that the Big Bang happened 12 billion years ago. But why did it happen? I don't just mean what sort of particles clashed to create the bang. I mean how did the particles get there in the first place? What was there before? And don't just say nothing, because that is unimaginable. Hard nothing? Soft nothing? A spacey sort of nothing? Scientists may one day be able to explain the mechanics of creation. But I cannot see how they will ever be able to explain the reason for it (if there was one) or the concepts of eternity and infinity.'

This bears out my own experience in talking to young people. They are fascinated by the concept of such things as infinity. The fact that, for instance, it is impossible to think of either the largest, or the smallest, possible number. At the end of the second millennium people are talking about religion, and opinion-formers are writing about it.

Utley goes on to make the point that a survey by the Brand Futures Group showed that 20 per cent of those defined as 'trend-setters' agreed with the proposition that religion played an important part in their lives. These were people identified as more open-minded and out-going than the rest; and it was a higher percentage than the rest of the population.

One of the reasons why the strong residue of Christian awareness has remained over the centuries is the English language. So many phrases from the Bible, the Book of Common Prayer, and *Hymns Ancient and Modern* are in almost daily use: scapegoat, prodigal son, fattened calf, Judas, lift up your hearts, out of the mouths of babes and sucklings, God willing. There is no greater canon of literature in common usage in the English tongue. That must be something the church builds on.

As indeed it is. Copies of a new Everyman's edition of the Book of Common Prayer are to be placed in every one of the 4300 state secondary schools, and a further 2000 distributed abroad by the British Council. Also, under the auspices of a campaign entitled JC 2000 and led by MP Andrew Rowe, schools will be encouraged to use the creative arts to examine the question, 'If Jesus of Nazareth came to your community in 2000, what would He say to you, and what would you say to Him?' Andrew Rowe explains the message they want to put across to schools is the need to put Christ back into the millennium:

> Wherever we look – at hospitals such as St Bartholomew's, at schools such as Westminster or St Peter's, York, at universities such as St Andrews or Queen's, Belfast – we see Christianity in their origins. Continuing sectarian violence in Ireland bears witness to some Christians' self-deception. But for all this, it is their efforts down the centuries that still shape our law, our democracy and a huge preponderance of our buildings and artefacts. I believe that our children are entitled to judge for themselves what that tradition means to them.

Interestingly enough at the end of the century it is still the church that is taking a great deal of the lead, by example; for instance in education, as they did at the start of the century. Places at church schools are in great demand – witness the many figures in public life who opt out of secular state schools in searching for secondary education for their own children. More church schools are going to be established. There may be complex reasons for this but the basic fact cannot be swept away. Parents are keen to send their children to church schools. If both church and state asked why, then perhaps lessons could be learnt which the church could offer the state.

This is a situation, together with the continuing interest in religion, which many would not have thought possible if asked to anticipate the place of the church in the year 2000 AD.

Perhaps the Church of England was slow to come to the millennium celebrations. Cardinal Basil Hume, the former Roman Catholic Archbishop of Westminster, encouraged the Archbishop of Canterbury to lead the prayers for the nation, saying that this was the moment for us to reflect on our society and the direction it is taking. Those words of encouragement from a Roman Catholic Archbishop to the leader of the Church of England demonstrate what vast strides we have taken in one aspect of inter-denominational unity. It wouldn't have been possible at the start of the century. An important factor of the Church of England's position as the established church is that in certain structural and constitutional areas it is able to speak for religion as a whole. In an agreed statement Lambeth Palace quotes, for the record, 'The Archbishop of Canterbury is seen by other faiths as a protector of their interests in this country and is happy to play that role.' This echoes the thoughts of the religious scholar T. Modood, who argues that establishment means the Church of England can act as a channel for all other denominations and faiths giving them access to decision-makers. He maintains that rather than thinking in terms of disestablishing the Church of England, to put it on the same status as others, it makes more practical sense for the established church to be there to help and improve the status of other churches and faiths.

Celebrations in the Church of England take place at all levels and the main millennium activities were organized at parish level with many parishes encouraging their members to display lighted candles in the windows of their homes. At international level the millennium has encouraged more concentrated activity by (and from) the Anglican–Roman Catholic International Commission, notably by holding the first ever conference in Toronto of all Anglican primates from the forty or so provinces and the leaders of the Roman Catholic Bishops' Conference. This was a direct result of face-to-face discussions between Pope John Paul II and the Archbishop of Canterbury in Rome in February 1999. Like international politicians, international priests are recognizing it is much easier to deal with problems by talking face to face than retreating backwards into one's own comfortable group.

There is one strong similarity between politicians and priests I have not yet touched on. They both want to change the world and make it better. They both announce and parade their views to the rest of the world. They both are prepared to stand up in the market place of ideas and risk being shouted down, abused, or made a fool of. They both have a certain amount of arrogance in that they think they 'know' what is best. That is a fairly high-risk position, so it is not surprising that from time to time both politicians and priests are toppled from their pedestals. Collectively this could be God's way of showing us that we are all vulnerable, especially if we fly too near the sun.

There have been many examples this century of the vulnerability – in churches and religions and in political parties. The tabloid press has made sure we know all the details. The broadsheets say it is disgusting that the gutter press prints these stories, then they publish the details themselves so we can exercise our judgement on how dreadful the tabloids are. Everybody 'tut tuts': television commentators, radio presenters, our neighbour over the garden wall, our friend at work, our pal in the pub, all agree it is disgraceful. It shouldn't be allowed to be published. The papers sell out. Marvellous hypocrisy!

Some cases like child abuse are tragic and serious; other cases are just examples of human weakness and frailty where we can all say, 'There but for the grace of God'. But because these lapses affect politicians and priests who set themselves up as examples of how we should live, it does attract interest when they fall. Are they more liable to fall than others, or do they just get the attention because of their work? There are different views on this. Matthew Parris, who wrote 'Great Parliamentary Scandals', found the sins of politicians humdrum compared with priests, and in *The Great Unfrocked*, he says: 'I cannot believe that a study of the sins of shipping clerks would have yielded as rich a harvest as we offer you here.' But sins there are in both professions.

As the millennium approaches it is worth making the point that it was ever thus. Charles James Fox, when a bankrupt Chancellor of the Exchequer, was accused by another MP: 'If I lived like you do I would either die of VD or swing at Traitors' Gate.' To which Fox replied: 'That, Sir, would depend on whether you embraced my mistress or my principles.'

Sex and money scandals occurred in the church as well. In *Crimes of the Clergy* (1823), William Benbow writes: 'Political, puritanical, proud, gambling, drunken, boxing and fox hunting parsons we have in abundance – who blazon their deeds to the world; but how few are really devout ministers, who act upon the doctrines laid down by our blessed Redeemer?'

I would put Matthew Parris's book on the reading list of all those wishing to be ordained, not just for light reading, but as a corrective to the sincere and earnest expression put to me once by a young man thinking about applying to be ordained. He said, 'I've visited lots of churches and talked to many clergy. I'm just not good enough.' Have this book by your bedside (among others I hasten to add!) for when you wake up worried in the dark watches of the night, and read the first paragraph:

> Many of the people in this book went to Oxford, and a large number of them were hanged. Nearly all were ordained priests or ministers, many were bishops, some were Archbishops, and one may have been the Pope. Some were formally unfrocked by Church authorities, others less ceremoniously disgraced. Most died ignominiously, or in the Rev. Harold Davidson's case, savaged by a lion in Skegness.

If the lifestyle of politics or the church is one in which troubles lie in wait, with attendant publicity for the unwary, it is also a lifestyle which offers the chance to help, inspire and indeed change the lives of others. There can be a heavy price to pay for personal failure, but the real rewards of success are truly awesome. Politicians will normally see their success more clearly in legislation or in action helping the lives of others. Priests may not see their rewards so clearly; but they may be more satisfying.

The lives, professions and work of both are inextricably bound together. Not only do they both have visions for a better future, the best of them are actively trying to bring about that future, knowing they will always fall short of the ideal in this life. To be effective they both need to be expert in the use of words, or, in the case of priests, in 'the Word'. That is why they must move from thoughts and prayers concerned with the visionary ideal to the mundane preparation of sermons and speeches. The medium of communication for politician and priest is very much the same.

It is not just words. There is a step further: planning, campaigning and lobbying to put the ideas the words express into reality. The politician uses the channels offered by political parties, town halls, the Palace of Westminster, and departments of government. The Christian, both clergy and laity, must use the channels they have – and if they are not sufficient, construct new ones, taking advantage of a country with an unwritten constitution, an uncensored internet and a media not controlled by whatever governing party is in power. For members of the Church of England it means using all the avenues that both the fact and the concept of establishment make available. For the leaders of the Church of England it means recognizing that some of their members feel the church does not do that – almost as though it is ashamed of being the nation's church. One priest said to me, 'I sometimes feel that there are some members, both clergy and laity, who look at the challenge of being a national established church and say, "We just can't cope. It's too big a responsibility."' This view was expressed by someone willing to be named, Dr Diane Greenwood, the retiring Director of Education in the Diocese of Rochester. In a speech quoted in *The Rochester Link* (June 1999), she said:

> I sometimes feel that the church has a treasury, an inheritance from past generations, which it does perhaps, just a tad, neglect: not make the best use of. It does appear to me that we have marvellous buildings, which we neglect or allow to fall down. We have a wonderful liturgy, which we replace with banality. We have an assured social and political position within our country, which we seem slightly ashamed of. This should not be our attitude, surely. We have been given these things, gift of God, act of providence, work of our noble and much more passionate ancestors.

A friend with whom I was discussing this book said that it wasn't very spiritual, and that was the real reason why people came to God. There are many inspiring spiritual books and it is partly through those, and thought and study and discussion that hopefully we grow in prayer which leads us to a greater understanding of the Will of God. Nothing can ever be complete in this life. But hopefully, that understanding will help us to be more effective in trying to be part of the Body of Christ on earth. God is Spirit, but God is timeless. God was made man in our historic understanding of chronological time. But, as God is timeless, God is also Man. Jesus said: 'When I was hungry you gave me food; when thirsty you gave me drink; when I was a stranger you took me into your home ... anything you did for one of my brothers here, however insignificant, you did for me' (Matthew 25: 35, 40).

Christians have a duty to try to be effective.

16

References and Research

THIS is not primarily an academic book and so I have shunned the use
of footnotes. There are two other reasons for this. I agree with Noel
Coward that where there is any flow of writing, it is enormously
irritating to have to break the line of sight and direct one's eyes to the
bottom of the page. He compared it with being interrupted by the
front-door bell while making love and having to go downstairs to
answer it. Secondly, the pressure on academics to publish scholarly
works – in universities it is a requirement for promotion – has resulted
in volumes being published with a proliferation of notes (not at the
foot of the page, but at the end of each chapter). It is as though more
footnotes equates with more worthy research. Many years ago, when
universities were somewhat different in character, the late Warden of
Goldsmiths, Sir Ross Chesterman, used gently to tease the College
Research Committee with Danny Kaye's remark, 'Pinch one person's
piece of work and it's called plagiarism; pinch a hundred and it's
called research.'

I have used comments and opinions from other people. In many
cases this has been as a result of various conversations and discussions
over the years. In other cases I have drawn from books, which I
happily acknowledge in the text and attach a full list here in case
others would like to refer to them.

Part of this book is concerned with how to go about campaigning
and lobbying and I would first list the political, parliamentary and
general books needed in this area. But human contact is as important.
A visit or a telephone call to your local public library is normally the
best starting-point. There are reference books and websites on
absolutely everything and in most cases your local librarians will
push you in the right direction.

If you become really involved then you need certain books to hand all the time. *Who's Who*, published each year, is a list of, among others, the tribal elders, decision-makers (but not all) and opinion-formers (certainly not all). It is expensive, so here is a tip. As a book of record it is published each year, but the changes are marginal – people die, new people enter. So there is a lot of old stock around. It is well worth phoning round libraries to ask if they have any out-of-date, unwanted copies they are willing to sell.

There are quite a few parliamentary reference books around. I find *The Times Guide to the House of Commons* essential. It is published by *The Times* after each general election and contains details of each constituency result with a photograph of the elected Member of Parliament. There is a list of the incoming Government and an analysis of both the campaign and voting behaviour.

Both these two paperback books are published quarterly:

Parliamentary Companion
PMS Publication Ltd
19 Douglas Street
London SW1P 4PA
tel: 0207 233 8283   fax: 0207 821 9352
e-mail: pmspublications@btinternet.co.

Vacher's Parliamentary Companion
Vacher's Publications
113 High Street
Berkhamstead
Herts HP4 2DJ
tel: 01442 876 135   fax: 01442 876 133
or at Parliamentary Bookshop
12 Bridge Street
London SW1A 2JX
tel: 0207 219 3890

They each list all Members of Parliament and their constituencies; all members of the House of Lords; all government ministers and spokesmen for the opposition and other parties. An account of the functions and responsibilities of ministers is given and all senior civil servants are listed; also listed is the membership of all Select Committees, Backbench Committees and All-Party Committees. There is a complete guide to every official body: executive agencies; public offices; embassies and High Commissions both here and abroad; names, addresses and telephone, fax and e-mail numbers of all parliamentary and political media.

If you make contact with either of the publications for particular information their organizations can supply you with: Commons and Lords Hansards; copies of bills; Standing Committee Hansard; Select Committee Reports; Command Papers, including State Papers, White Papers, Green Papers, and Reports of Royal Commissions; Acts of Parliament and Statutory Instruments; Citizens Charter documents and the Reports from the Parliamentary Office of Science and Technology.

The information is thorough and specialized. For example, if you wanted to make contact with those members of both Houses you thought would have an interest in Christian Fellowship and the relationship with the Council of Jews, in a matter of minutes you could look up the following information:

All-Party Subject Groups
Christian Fellowship: Chair, Simon Hughes (Lib Dem); Vice-Chair, Viscount Brentwood (Con); Secretary, Donald Anderson (Lab); Treasurer, Lord Archer of Sandwell (Lab).
Council of Christians and Jews: Joint Chairs, Roger Casale (Lab) and Sir Sydney Chapman (Con) and Kerry Pollard (Lab) and Dr Evan Harris (Lib Dem).
Council of Church: Chair, Colin Pickthall (Lab); Vice-Chair, Julian Brazier (Con); Treasurer, Lord Alton (Lib Dem).

Having identified the people who might be of use, you can find out more about them from *The Times Guide* and *Who's Who*. (Note that some groups are very specialized, for instance there are all-party groups on such subjects as 'Osteoporosis', 'Cider' and 'Derbyshire'.)

Another useful book, which again comes out yearly and so it is often possible to buy second-hand copies cheaply, is *Whitaker's Almanack* from J. Whitaker and Sons Ltd, 12 Dyott Street, London WC1A 1DF. This has been coming out annually since 1868. In addition to parliamentary information it gives the basic details in terms of statistics and constitution of every country in the world. It lists every major society, club and association in the UK, every charity and trade union, as well as details of the armed services. Importantly for anyone involved in campaigning, it lists the names and addresses of all national, local, weekly and Sunday newspapers, all the trade press and specialist and academic magazines and journals – as well as all the special-interest (such as women's) magazines and all general magazines. It lists the major television companies, broadcasting networks and local radio.

Most organizations who deal with matters of pubic affairs have information departments who can be contacted through the organization's headquarters. With particular reference to the subject of this book these addresses may be useful:

The House of Commons
London SWIA OAA
tel: 0207 219 3000
Information Office: 0207 219 4272
website: hhtp:/www.parliament.uk/

The House of Lords
London SWIA 0PW
tel: 0207 219 3000
Information: House 0207 219 3107
website: http:/www.parliament.uk/lords/

The Labour Party
Millbank Tower
Millbank
London SW1P 4GT
tel: 0207 802 1000   fax: 0207 802 1234

The Conservative Party
Conservative Central Office
32 Smith Square
London SWIP 3HH
tel: 0207 222 9000   fax: 0207 222 1135

English Liberal Democrats
4 Cowley Street
London SW1P 3NB
tel: 0207 222 7999   fax: 0207 799 2170

The General Synod – Secretariat
Church House (and bookshop)
Great Smith Street
London SW1P 3NZ
tel: 0207 898 1000

Lambeth Palace – Secretariat of the Archbishop of Canterbury
Lambeth Palace Road
London SE1 7JU
tel: 0207 928 8282

European Commission Office – Information – London
8 Storey's Gate
London SW1P 3AT
tel: 0207 973 1992

European Parliament Information Office
2 Queen Anne's Gate
London SW1H 9AA
tel: 0207 227 4300

The Commonwealth Secretariat
Marlborough House
Pall Mall
London SWIY 5HX
tel: 0207 839 3411

United Nations Information Centre
Millbank Tower (21st Floor)
Millbank
London SW1P 4QH
tel: 0207 630 1981   fax: 0207 976 6478

Prayer by John Powers: 'Teach Me'

THIS prayer was written by John Powers, Associate Retreat Director at the Holy Family Monastery, West Hartford, Connecticut, USA. It is taken from his book *If They Could Speak*.

Teach me something
about the God I do – and do not believe in.
I do not believe in a God who
enjoys human suffering
hates the world
refuses people fun
blesses corrupt authority
likes being feared
belongs to only one church or one class of people
can't laugh at foolish human mistakes
casts people into hell for all eternity for the slightest infraction of
    dogmatic rules
can't enjoy a baby crying in church
has been captured by philosophical concepts
is understood by those who refuse to love
is worshipped in church but is forgotten on the streets
believes sex is evil
promises pie only in the sky and not a slice today
provides middle-class comforts
chooses sides in war
gives the answers to life's mysteries only to a select few
demands large donations in exchange for eternal reward
can't transform every person with love
believes human nature is inherently corrupt
hides when men and women are in need
excludes from worship those who struggle from doubts, sexuality, or
    anger at the church

compromises the spirit for the letter of the law
proclaims, 'I'll get you someday.'
created humanity, but then left us to our own devices
ignores the promise to be with us to the end of time
whose name is not hope
is as small as I am.

Teach me to believe in God who is:
new life
everything we honestly love
full of surprises
faithful to every promise
eternally young
free to all who choose freely
within every person, regardless of race, faith or economic class
all good
sensitive to those who fail, sin and make mistakes
weak
the foundation of all
being crucified today
utterly beyond adequate description
always on the side of truth
laughing at funny human formalities and rituals
always ready to meet us more than halfway
pleased when people simply try
more than our narrow picture of perfection
alive in this world, not just waiting in another
that mysterious 'something' that helps us survive the
   loss of loved ones
more than the sum total of human achievement or wishes
beyond all
a personal reality, not just an impersonal force
concerned with justice more than good order
the creator who continues to create today
still teaching those willing to learn
the answer to evil
understanding when habits addict us
suffering in all who suffer
worrisome to those who desire to have power over others
self-revealing through all that is most human
light enough to brighten any darkness
still rising up in hope today.

(Reprinted, with permission, from *If They Could Speak: Ten Witnesses to the Passion of Jesus*, © 1990 by John D. Powers, published by Twenty-Third Publications, Mystic, Connecticut, USA)

Bibliography

THESE are some of the books I have found particularly useful and enjoyed reading in the area of 'Politics, Prayer and Parliament'. Some of them I have quoted from. There are of course many others, and with the knowledge explosion always gathering pace, these are increasing at a fast rate, as is the information on the Internet. So do browse. You never know what might turn up. A few years ago I was on a private retreat at St Julian's, near Horsham, in Sussex. On the first day I was wandering around their extensive library, noticing that there was only one other person there, hard at work, poring over books at a table by the window. I picked a book at random to read before evening prayers. It was by Monica Furlong. At prayers the deacon prayed for the two guests at St Julian's that week, 'David Rogers and Monica Furlong'. Yes, out of all the thousands of books I could have picked from the shelves I chose one of Monica Furlong's. A real case of Christian serendipity.

The Bible and The Book of Common Prayer

Appleton, George, *The Practice of Prayer* (Mowbray, 1979)
Blue, Lionel, *My Affair with Christianity* (Hodder, 1998)
Bonhoeffer, Dietrich, *Letters and Papers from Prison* (Collins, 1959)
Buchanan, Colin, *Cut the Connection: Disestablishment and the Church of England* (Darton, Longman & Todd, 1994)
Catherwood, Christopher, *Church History* (Hodder, 1998)
Cockerell, Michael, *Sources Close to the Prime Minister* (Macmillan, 1984)
Cornwell, Peter, *Church and Nation* (Blackwell, 1983)
Davie, G., *Religion in Britain since 1945* (Blackwell, 1994)
Gilling, John, *When You Pray* (Darton, Longman & Todd, 1978)
Godden, Rumer, *Spiritual Poems* (Hodder, 1996)
Graffius, Christopher, *Election '97: Christian View* (Hodder, 1997)

Gummer, John, with Eric Heffer and Alan Beith, *Faith in Politics* (SPCK, 1987)

Harries, Richard, *Is There a Gospel for the Rich?* (Mowbray, 1992)

Harries, Richard, *Turning to Prayer* (Mowbray, 1978)

Hollings, Michael, *Lord Teach Us to Pray* (McCrimmon, 1986)

Hollingsworth, Mark, *The Ultimate Spin Doctor* (Hodder, 1997)

Hunter, Leslie, *The English Church* (Penguin, 1966)

Johnston, D. A. Hunter, *Church, Synod, State and Crown* (Published privately in Bath and Wells Diocese)

Lee, R. S., *Your Growing Child and Religion* (Pelican, 1965)

Losada, Isabel, *New Habits: Today's Women who Choose to Become Nuns* (Hodder, 1999)

Lovell, Terry, *Number One Millbank* (HarperCollins, 1997)

MacArthur, Brian, *Twentieth Century Speeches* (Penguin, 1992)

Mayne, Michael, *Pray, Love, Remember* (Darton, Longman & Todd, 1998)

McCoby, S. (ed.), *British Political Tradition: The Radical Tradition* (Kaye, 1952)

McKenzie, R. T., *British Political Parties* (Heinemann, 1963)

Moyser, George, *Church and Politics Today* (T. & T. Clark, 1985)

Parrinder, Geoffrey, *Living Religions* (Pan, 1964)

Parris, Matthew, *The Great Unfrocked* (Robson, 1998)

Paxman, Jeremy, *Friends in High Places* (Michael Joseph, 1990)

Pelling, Henry (ed.), *British Political Tradition: The Challenge of Socialism* (A&C Black, 1954)

Powers, John, *If They Could Speak* (23rd Publications, 1990)

Purves, Libby, *Holy Smoke* (Hodder, 1998)

Quoist, Michel, *Prayers of Life* (Gill & Macmillan, 1954)

Ramsey, Michael, *Be Still and Know* (Fount, 1982)

Reid, Gavin, *Hope for the Church of England* (Kingsway, 1986)

Robertson, David, *Dictionary of Politics* (Penguin, 1997)

Robinson, John, *Honest to God* (SCM Press, 1963)

Robinson, John, *The New Reformation* (SCM Press, 1965)

Sheppard, David, *Bias to the Poor* (Hodder, 1983)

Smith, Delia, *A Journey into God* (Hodder, 1998)

Thompson, Jim, *Why God?* (Mowbray, 1997)

Wells, John, *The House of Lords* (Hodder, 1997)

White, R. J. (ed.), *British Political Tradition: The Conservative Tradition* (Kaye, 1950)

Whiteaker, Stafford, *The Good Retreat Guide* (Rider, 1991)

Wilkinson, Alan, *Christian Socialism* (SCM Press, 1999)

Winnifrith, Douglas P., *The Church in the Fighting Line* (Hodder, 1915)

Young, Hugo, *One of Us* (Macmillan, 1989)

Index